Holiness Voices

This book is
dedicated
to the Church,
our Lord's Bride
in preparation.

Holiness Voices

A Practical Theology of Holiness

Edited by H. Robert Cowles
and K. Neill Foster

CHRISTIAN PUBLICATIONS
CAMP HILL, PENNSYLVANIA

Christian Publications
3825 Hartzdale Drive, Camp Hill, PA 17011

Faithful, biblical publishing since 1883

ISBN: 0–87509–576–3
© 1995 by Christian Publications
LOC Catalog Card Number 95–68988
All rights reserved
Printed in the United States of America

95   96   97   98   99   5   4   3   2   1

Contents

Principles of Holiness

Holiness and the Fourfold Gospel

Perspectives on Holiness

Preface

*H*oliness Voices is a serious attempt to address a vital issue of our day. How should we Christians live in unholy times?

How should we live in view of the righteous demands of Scripture? For example: "Without holiness no one will see the Lord" (Hebrews 12:14). Or the words of God Himself: "Be holy, because I am holy" (Leviticus 11:45).

Indeed, how may sinful people find a compatible relationship with the infinitely Holy One?

We are aware that there is interest in this subject. Deep interest. For that reason, though all of the contributors relate to one fellowship in particular, The Christian and Missionary Alliance, we gladly, joyfully proffer these chapters to the worldwide body of Jesus Christ.

Nowhere is there a hint, on even one page, that personal acts of benevolence or good works will ever suffice.

It should soon become clear that none of the contributors has made exaggerated personal claims to holiness. You will quickly discover that you are in the presence of fellow pilgrims, all of whom have pressed hard in the pursuit of God.

Welcome to the journey!

K. Neill Foster, Publisher
Easter, 1995

Principles
of
Holiness

	Holiness Is
CHAPTER	**Not an**
1	**Option!**

by A.W. Tozer

As he who called you is holy, so be holy in all you do; for it is written: "Be holy, because I am holy." (1 Peter 1:15-16)

YOU CANNOT STUDY THE BIBLE diligently and earnestly without being struck by an obvious fact. The whole matter of personal holiness is highly important to God!

Neither do you have to give long study to the attitudes of present-day Christian believers to discern that by and large we consider the expression of true Christian holiness to be just a matter of personal option. "I have looked it over and considered it, but I don't buy it!"

I have always liked the word *exhort* better than *command*. So I remind you that Peter has given every Christian a forceful exhortation to holiness of life and conversation. He clearly bases this exhortation on two great facts—first, the character of God, and second, the command of God.

His argument comes out so simply that we sophisticates stumble over it: God's children ought to be holy because God Himself is holy! We so easily overlook the fact that Peter was an apostle. He is here confronting us with the force of an apostolic injunction. It is completely in line with the Old Testament truth concerning the person and character of God. It is also in line with what the Lord Jesus taught and revealed to His disciples and followers.

Personally, I am of the opinion that we who claim to be apostolic Christians do not have the privilege of ignoring such an apostolic injunction. I do not mean that a pastor can forbid or that a church can compel. I mean only that morally we dare not ignore this commandment, "Be holy."

We Cannot Ignore It

Because it is an apostolic word, we must face up to the fact that we will have to deal with it in some way. We cannot ignore it, as some Christians do.

Certainly no one has provided us with an option in this matter. We do not have the right to look into the Bible and say, "I am willing to consider this matter, and if I like it I will buy it"—using the language of the day.

Something is basically wrong with our Christianity and our spirituality if we can carelessly presume that no harm is done if we choose not to "buy" a biblical doctrine we do not like.

Commandments from our Lord or from the apostles we cannot overlook or ignore. God has never given us liberty to weigh His desires for us in the balances of our own judgment and decide what we want to do about them.

Of course you can walk out on God's commands! God has given every one of us the power to make our own choices. I am not saying that we are forced to bow our necks to God's yoke. It is true that if we do not like what God says, we can turn our backs.

It happened in Jesus' day. Many followed Him for a while and then walked away.

Jesus turned to those remaining and said, "You do not want to leave too, do you?" (John 6:67).

Peter gave the answer which is still my answer today: "Lord, to whom shall we go? You have the words of eternal life" (6:68).

Those were wise words, indeed—words born of love and devotion.

Forced to Make a Choice

So we are not forced to obey in the Christian life. But at many points in our spiritual journey we are forced to make a choice.

We have that power within us to reject God's instruction—but where else shall we go? If we refuse His words, which way will we turn? If we turn away from the authority of God's Word, to whose authority do we yield? Our mistake is that we generally turn to a human leader.

I am old-fashioned about the Word of God and its authority. I am committed to believe that if we ignore it or consider its commandments optional, we jeopardize our souls. We earn for ourselves severe judgment to come.

Now, I have said that the matter of holiness is highly important to God. I have personally counted in an exhaustive concordance and found that the word *holiness* occurs 650 times in the Bible. I have not counted words with a similar English meaning, such as *sanctify* and *sanctified,* so the count would jump nearer to a thousand if we counted these other words with similar meanings.

This word *holy* is used to describe the character of angels, the nature of heaven and the character of God. It is written that angels are holy and those angels who gaze down upon the scenes of humankind are called the watchers and holy ones.

It is said that heaven is a holy place where nothing unclean can enter. God Himself is described by the adjective *holy*—Holy Spirit, Holy Lord and Holy Lord God Almighty. These words are used of God throughout the Bible, showing that the highest adjective, the highest attribute that can be ascribed to God is that of holy. In a relative sense, even the angels in heaven partake of the holiness of God.

We note in the Bible, too, that "without holiness no one will see the Lord" (Hebrews 12:14). I am aware of some of the grotesque interpretations which have been given to that text. My position is this: I will not throw out this Bible text just because some people have misused it to support their own patented theory about holiness. This text does have a meaning and it ought to disturb us until we have discovered what it means and how we may meet its conditions.

What Does Holiness Really Mean?

What does this word *holiness* really mean? Is it a negative kind of piety from which so many people have shied away?

No, of course not! Holiness in the Bible means moral wholeness—a positive quality. Whenever the Scriptures declare God to be holy, they mean He is kind, merciful, pure and blameless with a white-heat intensity of degree. When used of people, it does not mean absolute holiness as it does of God, but it is still a positive—not negative—word.

True Bible holiness is positive—a holy man or woman can be trusted, can be tested. People who try to live by a negative standard of piety, a formula that has been copyrighted by other humans, will find that their piety does not stand up in times of difficult testing.

Genuine holiness can be put into the place of testing without fear. Whenever there is a breakdown of holiness, that is proof there never was any real degree of holiness in the first place.

I have been stirred in my heart by reading the accounts and testimonies of humble people of God whom I consider to be among the spiritual giants of Christian church history.

The word *holiness* did not at first have a primarily moral connotation. When applied to God, His morality was taken for granted! The root of the word referred to something beyond—to something strange and mysterious and awe-inspiring. When we consider the holiness of God we talk about something heavenly, awesome and mysterious. This is supreme when it relates to God, but it is also marked in people of God and deepens as they become more like God.

It is a sense of awareness of the other world, a mysterious quality and difference that has come to rest upon some people. Now, if a person should have that sense and not be morally right, then I would say that he or she is experiencing a counterfeit of the devil.

Whenever Satan has reason to fear a truth very gravely, he produces a counterfeit. He will try to put that truth in such a bad light that the very persons who are most eager to obey it are frightened away from it. Satan is very sly and very experienced in parodying truth which he fears the most. Then he pawns his parody off as the real thing and soon frightens away the serious-minded saints.

I regret to say that some who have called themselves by a kind of copyrighted holiness have allowed the doctrine to harden into a formula which has become a hindrance to repentance. Their doctrine has been invoked to cover up frivolity and covetousness, pride and worldliness.

I have seen the results. Serious, honest persons have turned away from the whole idea of holiness because of those who have claimed it and then lived selfish and conceited lives.

But we are still under the holy authority of the apostolic command. Men of God have reminded us in the Word that God does indeed ask us and expect us to be holy people of God, because we are the children of a holy God. The doctrine of holiness has been badly and often wounded. The provision of God through His pure, gentle and loving Spirit is still the positive answer for those who hunger and thirst for a life well-pleasing to God.

Let good people with this special quality and mysterious Presence be morally right. Let them walk in all the holy ways of God. Let them carry upon themselves without even knowing it the fragrance of a kingdom that is supreme above the kingdoms of this world. I am ready to accept such as being of God and from God!

The Illustration of Moses

By way of illustration, remember that Moses possessed these marks and qualities when he came down from the mount. He had been there with God 40 days and 40 nights. When he came back, everyone could tell where he had been. The lightning still played over his countenance, the glory of the Presence remained. This strange something which no one can pin down or identify was there.

I lament that this mysterious quality of holy Presence has all but forsaken the earth in our day. Theologians long ago referred to it as the "numinous." They meant that overplus of something that is more than righteous, but is righteous in a fearful, awesome, wondrous, heavenly sense. It is as though it is marked by brightness, glowing with a mysterious fire.

We Have Reduced God to Our Terms

I say this Presence has all but forsaken the earth, and I think the reason is very obvious. We are people who have reduced God to our own terms. In the context of the Christian church, we are now told to "gossip" the gospel and "sell" Jesus to people! We still talk about righteousness, but we are lacking in that bright quality, that numinous which is beyond description.

This mysterious fire was in the bush, as you will remember from the Old Testament. A small fire does not frighten people unless it spreads and gets out of control. We are not afraid of fire in that sense, yet we read how Moses, kneeling beside a bush where a small fire burned, hid his face for he was afraid! He had met that mysterious quality. He was full of awe before that manifested Presence.

Later, alone in the mountain and at the sounding

of a trumpet, Moses shook and said, "I am trembling with fear" (Hebrews 12:21).

We are drawn again and again to that Shekinah that was over Israel, for it sums up wonderfully this holiness of God's Presence. There was the overhanging cloud not made of water vapor, not casting a shadow anywhere, mysterious.

As the light of day would begin to fade, that cloud began to turn incandescent, and when the darkness had settled, it shone brightly like one vast light hanging over Israel.

Every tent in that diamond-shaped encampment was fully lighted by the strange Shekinah that hung over it. No man had built that fire. No one added any fuel—no one stoked or controlled it. It was God bringing Himself within the confines of the human eye and shining down in His Presence over Israel.

I can imagine a mother taking her little child by the hand to walk through the encampment.

I am sure she would kneel down and whisper to the little fellow: "I want to show you something wonderful. Look! Look at that!"

Probably his response would be, "What is it, Mama?"

Then she would reply in a hushed voice: "That is God—God is there! Our leader Moses saw that fire in the bush. Later, he saw that fire on the mountain. Since we left Egypt that fire of God has hovered over us all through these years."

"But how do you know it is God, Mama?"

"Because of the Presence in that fire, the mysterious Presence from another world."

This Shekinah, this Presence, had no particular connotation of morality for Israel—that was all taken for granted. It did connote reverence and awe, the solemn and inspiring, the different and wonderful and glorious. All of that was there.

Then it came down again at Pentecost—that same fire sitting upon each of them. It rested upon them with an invisible visibility. If there had been cameras, I do not think those tongues of fire could have been photographed—but they were there. It was the sense of being in or surrounded by this holy element. So strong was it that when the Christians gathered on Solomon's Colonnade of the temple, the people stood off from them as wolves will stand away from a bright camp fire. They looked on, but the Bible says, "No one else dared join them" (Acts 5:13).

Why? Were they held back by any prohibition or restriction?

No one had been warned not to come near these praying people, humble and harmless, clean and undefiled. But the crowd could not come. They could not rush in and trample the place down. They stood away from Solomon's Colonnade because they had sensed a holy quality, a mysterious and holy Presence within this company of believers.

Now, that kind of Presence emanates from God as all holiness emanates from God. If we are what we ought to be in Christ and by His Spirit, if the whole sum of our lives beginning with the inner life is becoming more Godlike and Christlike, I believe something of that divine and mysterious quality and Presence will be upon us.

Saints with Holy Brightness

I have met a few of God's saints who appeared to have this holy brightness upon them, but they did not know it because of their humility and gentleness of spirit. I do not hesitate to confess that my fellowship with them has meant more to me than all of the teaching I have ever received. I stand deeply indebted to every Bible teacher I have had through the years, but they did little but instruct my head. The people I have known who had this strange and mysterious quality and awareness of God's Person and Presence instructed my heart.

Do we understand what a gracious thing it is to be able to say of a person, "He is truly a man of God," or, "She is truly a woman of God"? The person doesn't have to tell us that. He or she lives quietly and confidently day by day with the sense of this mysterious, awesome Presence that comes down on some people. It means more than all the glib tongues in the world!

Actually, I am afraid of all the glib tongues. I am afraid of the man who can always flip open his Bible and answer every question. He knows too much! I am afraid of the person who has thought it all out and has a dozen epigrams he can quote. Over the years he has thought up answers to settle every spiritual question. I'm afraid of such a person!

There is a silence that can be more eloquent than all human speech. Sometimes there is a confusion of face and bowing of the head that speaks more divine truth than the most eloquent preacher can impart.

So, Peter reminds us that it is the Lord who has said, "Be holy, because I am holy."

First, bring your life into line morally so that God can make it holy. Then bring your spiritual life into line that God may settle upon you with the Holy Spirit—with that quality of the Wonderful and the

Mysterious and the Divine.

You do not cultivate it and you do not even know it, but it is there and it is this quality of humility invaded by the Presence of God which the church of our day lacks. Oh, that we might yearn for the knowledge and Presence of God in our lives from moment to moment! Oh, that without human cultivation and without toilsome seeking there would come upon us this enduement that gives meaning to our witness! It is a sweet and radiant fragrance and I suggest that in some of our churches it may be strongly sensed and felt.

Now that I have said that, I had better stop and predict that some will ask me, "You don't go by your feelings, do you, Mr. Tozer?"

Well, I do not dismiss the matter of feeling and you can quote me on that if it is worth it!

Feeling is an organ of knowledge and I do not hesitate to say so. Feeling is an organ of knowledge.

Will you define the word *love* for me? I don't believe you can actually define love. You can describe it but you cannot define it. A person or a group of people or a race which has never heard of love can never come to an understanding of what it is even if they could memorize the definitions in all the world's dictionaries.

But just consider what happens to any simple, freckle-faced boy with his big ears and his red hair awry when he first falls in love. At once he knows more about love than all of the dictionaries put together!

This is what I am saying—love can be understood only by feeling it. The same is true with the warmth of the sun. Tell a man who has no feeling that it is a warm day and he will never understand what you

21

mean. But take a normal man who is out in the warm sun and he will soon know it is warm. You can know more about the sun by feeling that you can by description.

So there are qualities in God that can never be explained to the intellect and can only be known by the heart, the innermost part of our being. That is why I say that I believe in feeling. I believe in what the old writers called "religious affection"; we have so little of it because we have not laid the groundwork for it. The groundwork is repentance and obedience and separation and holy living!

I am confident that whenever this groundwork is laid, there will come to us this sense of the otherworldly Presence of God and it will become wonderfully, wonderfully real.

I have at times heard an expression in our prayers, "Oh, God, draw feelingly near!"

I don't think that God is too far off—in spite of those who can only draw back and sit in judgment.

"Oh, God, come feelingly near!" God drew feelingly near to Moses in the bush and on the mount. He came feelingly near to the church at Pentecost.

I am willing to confess in humility that we need this in our day.

CHAPTER	Holiness:
2	"Let Us Draw Near"

by David L. Rambo

THERE IS A PROBLEM THAT dogs the life of almost every Christian, including pastors, missionaries, and denominational leaders. The matter, simply put, is this: *Christians—even the best who magnificently serve the Lord—live day by day and year by year without a close, intimate relationship with God as the wellspring of their lives.* God seems a distant Presence, prayer to Him a chore, and intimacy with Him an elusive and frustrating non-happening.

Some have more or less given up on knowing God intimately. They have responded time and time again to sermons, books and numerous invitations. Having responded, they experience a short period of closeness with Christ. Their prayer life surges for a time and they sing, "He walks with me and He talks with me."

But alas, in a period of days or weeks, Christ grows increasingly remote. With each such experience, their souls become scorched, and they succumb to the belief that only a chosen few seem able to overcome the barriers to walking with God. The conclusion is that if nearness to God is possible at all, for whatever reason, it may be reserved for someone else. They take the blame and settle for a distant relationship—often unwittingly.

In place of intimacy with God, other Christians are content to be a casual acquaintance, keeping the relationship superficial. Somewhere along the way, they took God aboard, but the two seldom talk or spend time together. They experience God more as a friendly stranger than a close companion.

Most of us, however, have not settled for having God as a tack-on acquaintance. We want to know Him better. But in all honesty, we have found Him rather hard to know. We have little trouble working for Him, but like a corporate boss, He sets high standards for a friendship. He often acts strangely, even appearing not to act at all. When we talk with Him, it seems as if He is not always listening. He is there, but not really there.

Total Intimacy Deferred

Because God is God, we think it blasphemous even to entertain the thought that some of our difficulty in establishing intimacy may rest not with us but with God Himself. Like a battered wife, or an abused child, we have concluded that the problem is all our fault. Yet taking all the blame for our superficial relationship may in fact be part of the problem.

I realize that I may be introducing some uncomfortable thoughts, though I contend biblical ones. First, let me remind you that it is not God's purpose that we know Him perfectly here below. Complete intimacy with the Almighty is not attainable in this life.

Isaiah was a man who experienced God like few people have ever known Him. "Holy, holy, holy is the LORD Almighty. . . . Woe to me! . . . For I am a man of unclean lips, and I live among a people of unclean lips," he cried (see Isaiah 6:3,5). Yet, he is the one who discovered that God's thoughts are not our thoughts and His ways are not ours (Isaiah 55:8).

Simply spoken, the Almighty will always be on a different wavelength than we are. Try as we might, work at it as we can, God is God and complete intimacy with Him is reserved for the life to come. Then, and only then, we will know God as we are known by Him. Then, and only then, we shall be like Him because we will see Him as He really is. Now, we see Him through a cloudy mirror. Then, we shall know Him face to face.

That message—utterly biblical—flies in the face of a perfectionism suggesting that God can be fully known in this life. If we strive hard enough, we can enter the inner sanctum of the Almighty. I suggest that one reason for our spiritual frustration is that—with the best of intentions—our hopes have been raised too high, contributing to spiritual disillusionment. We have been promised here and now a level of intimacy that God has reserved for the life beyond.

Has God Seemed to Let You Down?

Steve Seamonds in his magnificent new book, *A Conversation with Jesus,* tells of a student bold enough to express his pent-up anger with God. He said his dad always put pressure on him to excel in sports. One night his father—in a rare appearance—went to see his son play. His son, knowing his father was there, played the game of his life, scoring 29 points, an all-time personal high. He could hardly wait to get home, knowing how proud his father would be. When he arrived, his father said, "You played a good game, son," but then proceeded to tell him five or six ways he could have done better. It's difficult to experience intimacy with God when we perceive Him as always saying, "You scored 29 points, but I think you could have done better."

Seamonds also tells about a student who, in an emotional cloudburst, told this story:

> About five years ago, my wife left me. That came as a great shock—I never thought this could happen to me. Yet, I was sure God would not allow our separation to continue. . . . So I prayed and I prayed because I was sure God was going to come through. But He didn't. And now I'm afraid to trust God with anything in my life. I've been burned once; I don't want to be burned again.

When we feel abandoned by God, it is extremely difficult to draw near to Him. Last year, during a service focused on divine healing for the body, my dear friend, Paul Bubna, asked me to pray and anoint his wife, Jeanie. I did so with a heavy heart and tears in my eyes, begging the Almighty to have mercy and to heal. Later, I looked into her open grave and felt the sting of an unanswered prayer.

We Must Allow God to Be God

I know all the answers you may want to give to rescue God and me. But please save them. In the experience I'm learning something about God and how to know Him. I'm learning that one irreplaceable ingredient in any relationship of intimacy is to allow the other person to act on his or her own. To impose our expectations on how the other must act is the archenemy of intimacy. If I should insist that I set the terms for the relationship, I cannot attain intimacy. Only as the one is released to act apart from the expectations of the other can closeness take place.

Every married person instinctively knows this. To impose our will on our spouse as a condition for intimacy destroys a marriage. And with God, I must not impose my frail understanding on His omniscience. Thus, Jeanie is gone, and I don't know why. I'll allow God to keep it a secret and not make it a condition for friendship. If I would be near to God, I must allow Him to say "No" to my prayers.

The Latin fathers called it *Deus abconditius*, the part of God and His purposes that we will never know. To experience God intimately requires that we not insist on His telling us all His secrets or acting according to our formulas.

I have spoken frankly about our problems in knowing intimacy with God. I am emboldened to do so because I believe that some of these problems of unrealistic expectations and frozen anger with God—often deeply hidden in spiritual language—are at the heart of the problem.

Divinely Desired Intimacy

The expectation that we can know God perfectly, or the belief that every encounter must be filled with ecstasy, or the perception that God keeps saying we could do better are destroyers of intimacy. We may never achieve a realistic closeness to God until our thinking and expectations are dismantled and rebuilt. The happy message of Scripture is that they can be and that God has taken the initiative to make it possible. Intimacy with us is extremely important to Him and therefore He has taken lavish steps to clear away the barriers.

The message began at creation. God, completely satisfied with the world He created, was nonetheless unfulfilled by the mountains, the rivers and even the menagerie of cleverly designed animals He created. God made us, the Genesis story recounts, "in His image," meaning that humankind stands a breed apart from the rest of His creation. Whatever "in His image" means, it certainly means that there is something inside of God that He placed inside of us.

God not only created us with a capacity to know Him but took the initiative to make it happen. That is an irreplaceable building block in our understanding of intimacy with God. We were created with the capacity to know Him and He took the initiative to make it happen. It was not humankind who sought the relationship in Eden. God wants that relationship much more then we. It is not the case of our clumsily trying to engage the Creator. It is God relentlessly pursuing us.

The second important thing is that God did not cut off the relationship. It was Adam and Eve who hid themselves and covered themselves because they broke the agreement by entertaining the notion that they could become like God. God did not run away. They did, and we have been doing so ever since.

Intimacy Resisted

It is God who comes in the cool of the day and seeks an intimate relationship with mortals. But time after time we have hidden ourselves, covering ourselves with the leaves of busyness and higher priorities and downright stubbornness.

What is the problem? Why is this the Achilles heel of every servant of God? Why is this the maddening frustration of nearly every honest Christian we know?

The answer is that we resist, even fear, intimacy. Ask any wife what she desires most from her husband. The answer is closeness—his opening the inner sanctum and allowing his wife in. But there is something utterly terrifying about being known. While we wistfully like the idea of intimacy, it is a fearful, unnerving prospect.

Deep down inside, we hide our fears, our feelings of worthlessness, our inner secrets of weakness. They are buried beneath the exterior of bravado and total control. Only we are aware of our weakness. We throw up walls hoping to keep our secrets intact. We fear if anyone knows who we really are, they will reject us—at least think less of us. If they know about our jealousies, our lustful passions, the deadness of our souls, they would ostracize us. If they knew how little we prayed, they might have no confidence in our leadership.

So we project a strong exterior self—one which we sense would be more acceptable to people. We can project happiness when we are sad inside, courage when we're scared to death and success even when things internally are falling apart.

We Become Unknowable

Soon we come to believe that this is really who we are—though we know it isn't. We become unknowable, not certain even who we are, and bring that unknowable self to our relationship to God. How can we expect intimacy when we bring a pseudo-self to Him? That was the problem of the Pharisee who prayed in the temple.

You see, God wants to know the real person within, not the "us" we parade in public. The hymnist had it right:

> Just as I am without one plea
> But that Thy blood was shed for me
> And that Thou bidd'st me come to Thee—
> O Lamb of God, I come.

That's the story of redemption. The God who was invisible, untouchable Spirit, realized it was difficult for us to know Him. So "the Word became flesh and made his dwelling among us" (John 1:14). Now we could see and feel and experience God come in human form. This same Jesus descended into the jaws of death to remove the barriers to intimacy. He who knew no sin became sin for us. He is the One who entered the strong man's house and put to death the very thing that keeps God at bay. By the blood of Christ, we have been brought near.

What Mattered Most to Paul

In this context Paul summarized what was important to him. He was growing older. He had more days behind him than ahead. He had seen the then-known world. He had intimately walked with his Lord. Now he is again in prison and takes pen in hand to express what is of utmost importance to him.

Though Paul won many to Christ, his chief desire is not to win more. Though he planted a dozen churches, his desire is not to plant a dozen more. His life's ambition is not to serve Christ better. Instead he writes:

> *I consider everything a loss compared to the surpassing greatness of knowing Christ Jesus my Lord.* (Philippians 3:8)

Herein lie important clues about intimacy with God. First, Paul was consumed with a desire to know Him. It was the most important pursuit of his life. He wanted to know God and was willing to lay out his life as an open book before Him. His life was transformed by Jesus on that fateful trip to Damascus. His relationship to Jesus changed radically from a relationship of utter hostility to one of intimacy.

Yet Paul understood that nearness to God did not just happen.

> *Not that I have already obtained all this, or have already been made perfect, but I press on to take hold of that for which Christ Jesus took hold of me.* (Philippians 3:12)

Paul was on a lifelong pursuit of knowing God.

Steps to Intimacy

I see both in the Word of God and in our Christian human experience three steps to intimacy with God. Here they are.

Step 1. The Power of His Resurrection. The apostle understood that in order to know Jesus, he had to walk with Jesus through the most joyous and painful experiences of life. As A.B. Simpson would say, he had to live the Christ-life.

To know Christ means to receive the power that motivated Jesus throughout His life. That power—which Paul says we too can have—is best demonstrated in Jesus' resurrection from the dead. That same power that brought Jesus from death to life brings us from spiritual death to spiritual life. When we were spiritually dead, separated from God, we neither experienced nor wanted to know intimacy with the Almighty.

Jesus took the blame for the separation when He bore our sins on the cross. On Easter morning, He rose from the dead, freeing us to know God. For that promise to become reality, Paul said, we need to receive His resurrection power. So we exclaim with Paul that the first thing we desire is to know Him. That is the irreplaceable first step to intimacy with God. "You will seek me and find me when you seek me with all your heart" (Jeremiah 29:13).

Then follows the experience of our own death—death to the insidious drives for success, for recognition, for taking charge, for pigheaded willfulness. Resurrection life begins with Good Friday. I need to die to "me" in order to be resurrected with Christ. Death to self is prologue to resurrection.

Steps Two and Three

Step 2. The Fellowship of His Sufferings. Knowing God also includes suffering. Jesus' life, need I say, was full of suffering. We can't know Him intimately apart from pain.

The apostle, ever in relentless pursuit of God, challenges us to walk through Jesus' pain. He beckons us to share in the rejection of the One who came to His own and His own would not accept Him. To walk with Him when even His best friends didn't know what He was trying to do. To hear the painful curse of a friend who, in order to save his skin, cried, "I never knew this Man."

"Pain," C.S. Lewis says, "is God's megaphone shouting messages that, in the noise of life, we are not able to hear." To know Christ intimately is to experience His pain.

Step 3. Made Like Him in His Death. Jesus lived a magnificent life, but in His death He truly shone. Remember Passion Week? The same people who in all probability had become hoarse by shouting "Hosanna" still had laryngitis when they began shouting "Crucify Him!" And Jesus went through the deepest of pain and rejection when people who should have stood up for Him fled.

When they nailed Him on the cross, I think more hurtful than the spikes was a sign put there by Pilate. It was written in derision, not to tell the truth. But it was a truthful sign: "This is Jesus, the King of the Jews." From the cross, He was still able to pray, "Father, forgive them. They don't know what they're doing." And I want to jump in and yell, "Yes, they did!" They knew what they were doing, but somehow, though hanging on the cross, Jesus responded with grace.

Then came the worst of all. God Himself—His Father—seemed to take away His smile. In His anguish He cries out, "You too, God? My God, why have you forsaken me?" (Mark 15:34).

He is asking us to walk the road. It is a journey, not some wonderful cataclysmic event, good as it may be. It is a day-to-day walk through Passion Week, experiencing the grace and love and forgiveness of what Jesus has done.

Conclusion

"That's the way I want to live," says Paul. "After all, it's the only thing that really matters" (see Philippians 3:8-14). It is true that we will never know Christ perfectly, but we can certainly know Him better—much, much better.

And we can enter into the Christ-life by faith—not simply living for Christ, important as that is, but responding to a God who waits for us to say, *I want to know Him.*

Intimacy with God involves all of that. But the wonderful thing is, depraved as we are, as reluctant as we are to have our meetings with God and despite the number of times that we break our appointments with Him, He is still seeking us. Is it important for you to know Him?

The key to the work of God is not to get busy saints busier, not to serve God harder when we're running on empty. It is to die to ourselves and to be raised to walk in newness of life. The key is to glorify God and enjoy Him forever—*intimately!*

34

CHAPTER	Holiness:
3	Our
	Calling

by Arnold L. Cook

THE CURRENT EVANGELICAL PASSION FOR relevance struggles with the term *holiness*. Attempts to substitute *integrity* or *purity* fail to convey the essence of God's intent. Peter puts it bluntly, quoting God Himself: "Just as he who called you is holy, so be holy in all you do; for it is written: 'Be holy, because I am holy'" (1 Peter 1:15, quoting God's words from Leviticus 11:44-45).

The concept *holiness* resists all dynamic equivalents because it is an attribute of God. In fact, it appears to be the most prominent aspect of His nature, if indeed God's character has any priority structure. Isaiah heard the seraphs calling to one another, "Holy, holy, holy is the LORD Almighty" (Isaiah 6:3). Not even God's love gets that emphasis.

As God's children, we have been the recipients of many callings. Different periods of church history, in divergent times and climes, have focused on different ones of these callings. In these waning years of the current millennium, for example, Church

Growth advocates have called the evangelical church to world evangelization. This has been a most timely call, despite our North American tendency to market good strategies into an obsession.

"Power evangelism," characterized by signs, wonders and miracles, properly calls us back to dynamic evangelism and the Great Commission. With it has come an overdue recovery of the "believer's authority" and the believer's role in spiritual warfare.

A plethora of other callings, each claiming biblical support, has distracted evangelicals from their call to be holy. The name-it-claim-it, health-and-wealth advocates have subtly duped many into unholy lifestyles. The Moral Majority briefly had evangelicals expending too much of their energy on political goals.

With such a multiplicity of voices, where does our calling to holiness fit in? I see four truths in the Scriptures regarding our call to holiness.

Holiness Is Our First Calling

The term *holy* appears 683 times in the Old Testament. Many of those are in Leviticus. On at least three occasions in that book (Leviticus 11:44, 45; 19:2), God says, "Be holy because I, the LORD your God, am holy."

The word *holy* occurs 78 times in the New Testament. And that is excluding the numerous references to the Holy Spirit.

We are admonished to be just, loving, honest, merciful—all virtues reflecting the nature of God. But our *call* is to be holy. God expresses it with an intentionality that sets it apart as our first calling among many.

God's multiple calls can be divided into two categories. Many have a focus on *doing*. At the beginning He commanded His human creation to "increase in number," to "subdue" the earth and to "rule over the fish . . . and the birds . . . and every living creature that moves on the ground" (Genesis 1:28). This is sometimes referred to as our cultural mandate.

At the end of Christ's ministry on earth, He called His apostles—and through them every member of His church—to "make disciples of all nations" (Matthew 28:19). But He made it abundantly clear that "being" must precede "doing." He admonished them, "Stay in the city until you have been clothed with power from on high" (Luke 24:49). It is parallel to Isaiah's experience. First he allowed God to purge his unholiness. Then he was ready to volunteer, "Here am I. Send me!" (Isaiah 6:6-8).

In the preface to his book, *Let the Nations Be Glad: The Supremacy of God in Missions,* John Piper distinguishes succinctly and well these two callings. "Missions is not the ultimate goal of the church," he says. "Worship is. Missions exists because worship doesn't."

Holiness Is Our High Calling

In the context of God's disciplining of us, His children, the writer of Hebrews reminds us of one of God's purposes: "God disciplines us for our good, that we may share in his holiness" (Hebrews 12:10). Peter explains how Christ's "divine power has given us everything we need for life and godliness" (2 Peter 1:3). Through His "glory and goodness" Christ "has given us his very great and precious promises, so that through them [we] may participate in the divine nature" (1:4).

How special is this? I am informed that the term *holiness* is foreign to every language. That should not surprise us. Its root meaning is "to cut, to separate." To be holy is to be "other." This reminds us of what we already profess: Our God is totally "other." He is transcendent. He exceeds the normal limits. He is utterly above the realm of this world order. And we earthlings have the high privilege to share that divine nature. Indeed, ours is a high calling.

As we noted earlier, Leviticus, God's guidebook for His newly redeemed nation of Israel, repeatedly articulates God's standard: "Be holy, for I am holy." Throughout the book, God makes frequent reference to holy places and holy things. Then He foreshadows the New Covenant, declaring, "I am the LORD, *who makes you holy*" (20:7, emphasis added).

This holiness became reality in the New Testament church. Paul could address the less-than-pious Corinthians in these optimistic terms: "To the church of God in Corinth, to those sanctified in Christ Jesus and called to be holy" (1 Corinthians 1:2).

Holiness is the highest calling any of us will ever experience. We are privileged to "share divinity." We are privileged to become like God.

Holiness Is an Endangered Calling

There is no agenda more important for the Christian than holiness. Nor is there a Christian experience in our day more in danger of being lost. Floyd McClung, a missions leader, in his book *Holiness and the Spirit of the Age*, warns: "Though the world in which we live has changed, it is plain that the sins of the flesh have not. Pleasures seduce us at every turn; selfish desires cry out for fulfillment. Yet in the midst of ever-increasing decay, God calls us to be holy."

The sins of the flesh threaten our spiritual lives as realistically as the untamed lions threatened Daniel's physical safety. Four of these sins are enumerated in Hebrews 12:

Missing the grace of God (12:15). Throughout his letter the writer has been concerned for those who "fall away" (6:6). This penchant of the flesh to back off from the sanctifying process of God's discipline is ever with us.

A root of bitterness (12:15). The reference is to a "bitter herb" used to concoct a poisonous drug. Bitterness is the most contagious of all the sins of the flesh. L.E. Maxwell, long time principal of Prairie Bible Institute, once warned a group of missionaries: "Beware lest your service sour as it lengthens."

Sexual immorality (see 12:16). We wonder how immorality could get more pervasive. But 20th century technology has done the impossible. No sin of the flesh is as blatantly contrary to holiness. Our bodies are the temples of the Holy Spirit. It is for this reason that God places sexual sin in a special category (see 1 Corinthians 6:18-20) and clearly enunciates its devastating effects.

Ungodliness (12:16). The term can also mean *carelessness*. Esau mindlessly sold his birthright for a bowl of soup. Esau lacked spiritual discernment. He lacked discipline. Discipline is the solid double line on the highway of holiness. We ignore it to our peril.

Holiness Is an Attainable Calling

Holiness can be as elusive as humility. When we think we have attained it, we have just lost it! John Wesley testified, "The closer I get to God, the farther I have to go." It is good to remember that God alone evaluates our progress.

Can we possibly attain our first calling, our high calling, our endangered calling? Take heart from what God says through the apostle Paul:

> *May God himself, the God of peace, sanctify you through and through. May your whole spirit, soul and body be kept blameless at the coming of our Lord Jesus Christ.* (1 Thessalonians 5:23)

And note the promise in verse 24:

> *The one who calls you is faithful and he will do it.*

How important is holiness? Important enough that we should "make every effort . . . to be holy" (Hebrews 12:14). How important is holiness? "Without holiness no one will see the Lord" (same verse).

Many ask, "How in this world can I be holy?" A.B. Simpson went to Colossians 1:27 for a simple yet profound answer, one that is totally, totally scriptural: "Christ in you, the hope of glory." It is one of those "precious promises" Peter mentions in his second Letter, "that through them you may participate in the divine nature and escape the corruption in the world caused by evil desires" (1:4). Holiness is escaping the corruption in the world.

Fall on the Ontario farm was potato picking time. With hoes and shovels we worked in the mud to harvest potatoes. Although the work memories of those days are not pleasant, one helpful analogy remains with me.

Occasionally I miscalculated. With my hoe I would slice open a potato. Always that potato was surrounded by slime, mud, dirt. But always the inside was completely white and pure—totally protected from the corrupting influences of its environment.

We are hidden with Christ, in God, and indwelt by the Holy Spirit.

We live Christ-like because we have the Christ-life. God is not satisfied with anything less than perfection. He required that from His Son. He requires it from us, and He does not, in the process of grace, reduce the standard. Instead, He brings us up to it. . . . He imparts it to us. . . . Lord, live out Thy very life in me.
—A.B. Simpson—

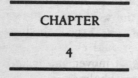

CHAPTER

4

The Holiness Movement

by Keith M. Bailey

THE QUEST FOR HEART PURITY is as old as the church. In every generation there have been some who proclaimed the possibility of victory over sin. During the Middle Ages the Friends of God were the voice of holiness. After the Reformation, the Pietists and later the Anabaptists called the church to a holy walk.

The contemporary holiness movement had its roots in Methodism. The Spirit-anointed preaching of John Wesley and his associates brought about a moral rebirth in England. The vitality of the Wesleyan revival was soon transplanted into Britain's colonies in North America.

The Wesleyan Legacy

Wesley preached the direct and immediate work of the Holy Spirit in conversion and, subsequently, in the believer's sanctification. He called for nonconformity to the world and holiness in day-to-day life.

In the New World, the revivals of the colonial

period kept alive the interest in holiness, but by the time of independence the spiritual temperature had cooled. Moral decline had set in. Once again, nationwide revival renewed the interest of Wesleyans and non-Wesleyans in holiness. The revival of 1859 refired the flames of holiness in the Methodist church and deeply stirred most mainline denominations. It was the hunger for holiness among non-Wesleyans that would eventually give birth to a transdenominational movement devoted to the proclamation of scriptural holiness.

How this movement came about is a fascinating story. In 1837 a young New York City doctor and his wife, Walter and Phoebe Palmer, came into the experience of sanctification. Wanting to share their transforming experience with those outside their own Methodist church, they opened their home on Tuesday mornings to interested people. The format was simple: testimony, prayer, instruction.

The home meetings soon became a movement made up not only of Wesleyans but of many from other churches who had embraced this "full salvation" teaching.

Their first national camp meeting was held in 1867 in Vineland, New Jersey. It was a landmark event. Thousands gathered for it, and in that convocation the National Holiness Camp Meeting Association (NHCMA) had its birth.

They held a second camp meeting in Lancaster County, Pennsylvania. Twenty-five thousand people attended, drawn by a desire for a pure heart and the baptism of the Holy Spirit. People from all denominations were there.

Through the 1870s, these holiness camp meetings prospered across the country. The Methodist bishops were concerned about the NHCMA's inter-denominational nature, but they endorsed it by their attendance at the camps. The spiritual vitality of the movement was obvious to all. It was a major spiritual awakening touching tens of thousands of Christians in America.

The "Higher Life" Movement

Many in the movement who experienced sanctification were not prepared to embrace the Wesleyan theological system. By 1880, leading Wesleyans were writing defenses of "pure" Wesleyan holiness and pointing out imagined weaknesses in the non-Wesleyan position.

The publication in 1858 of W.E. Boardman's *The Higher Christian Life* was a turning point for this new movement. Boardman, a Presbyterian who came to know Christ as his Sanctifier through some Methodist friends, began an itinerant ministry preaching sanctification. In his book Boardman put holiness in non-technical terms. While the NHCMA continued with great blessing, a new format was developing to promote this truth among Christians everywhere.

Conventions were called in New York, Philadelphia and other major cities to preach what non-Wesleyans called the "Higher Life," using Boardman's term. Thousands attended these conferences and carried the blessing of full salvation back to their home churches. Outstanding laypeople and pastors, testifying to their own experiences of sanctification, added credibility to the movement. Harriet Beecher Stowe, famed author of *Uncle Tom's Cabin*, was a devoted follower of the

Higher Life movement.

This new outpouring of spiritual power soon had the attention of the church across America. Local churches were revived. Evangelism became a priority. There was renewed commitment to overseas missions.

The Higher Life Spreads Overseas

Copies of Boardman's book were read as eagerly in England as in North America. In 1873 Boardman visited England. The result was a great interest in England and Europe in the Higher Life.

Two other leading lights of the movement also made a preaching tour of England: Robert Pearsall Smith and his even better known wife, Hannah Whitall Smith. Some leading Anglican ministers and laypeople accepted the Higher Life teachings and soon began plans for a major holiness conference in England.

Invitations went out not only to church people in England but to many in Europe and America as well. The roster of speakers read like a Who's Who of outstanding evangelical leaders. The Union Meeting for the Promotion of Scriptural Holiness opened August 29, 1874, at Oxford. Theodore Monod of the French Free Church, Otto Stockmayer of Switzerland and Theodore Jellinghaus of Germany as well as the Dean of Canterbury were in attendance. For eight days the large group waited on God and drank in the powerful preaching of Pearsall Smith, Boardman, Asa Mahan, William Arthur, Stockmayer, Evan H. Hopkins, Monod and others. The results must be described in terms of revival.

The following spring Pearsall Smith went to

Europe and preached holiness to thousands in Switzerland, Germany and France. The meetings had a lasting effect. One German church historian said the holiness movement gave a major thrust to evangelism throughout Germany.

Crisis in the Movement

In England, a second union meeting was called for 1875 in Brighton. Again, an international audience gathered to hear the Higher Life message. After the Brighton convocation, some leaders determined to hold a second conference a few months later, at Keswick. They booked Pearsall Smith to speak.

The Keswick conference was hardly announced when Smith and his wife suddenly left England for America. The reason was soon public knowledge. Smith had been guilty of an indiscretion. It was a blow to the Higher Life movement in England. Some wanted to cancel the conference, but the leaders determined to go through with it.

Keswick became, in fact, a turning point in the Higher Life movement in England. This branch of the movement continues to this day as a vital voice for holiness.

Not everyone joined forces with Keswick. Boardman centered his ministry in Bethshan in London. A number of regional conferences established in the beginning of the holiness movement in England continued their ministries without any formal association with Keswick.

The Historic Bethshan Conference

As the Higher Life movement gained momentum across North America, Britain and Western Europe, the doctrine of divine healing was enjoying widespread renewal. It, too, was transdenominational.

Divine healing turns up in the written records of the major holiness conferences, not in formal sermons but in testimonies of healing. Gradually there developed a sizeable group within the Higher Life movement who associated holiness and healing.

Ten years after Brighton, Boardman called a conference on divine healing and holiness to convene June 1, 1885, at Bethshan, London. An American minister, A.B. Simpson, was to speak at the conference. Four years earlier Simpson, fully convinced of both healing and holiness, had resigned his Presbyterian credentials to launch the Gospel Tabernacle in New York City.

The heart of the Higher Life position on sanctification was the fullness of Christ. Many were coming to understand that fullness in terms of justification, sanctification and healing for the body. In one of Simpson's sermons at Bethshan he emphasized also the return to earth of the Lord Jesus Christ as an integral part of the Higher Life message. In addition, the theme of worldwide missions kept emerging at that historic conference.

Bethshan was a step ahead of Keswick in the Higher Life movement. For years Keswick leaders refused to permit any presentation of missions, fearing it would detract from the holiness emphasis. The Bethshan group understood that a people walking in the fullness of Jesus would yearn to reach a lost world with the gospel.

The non-Wesleyan transdenominational holiness movement had come to maturity. It was to have its best years between 1885 and the end of the 19th century. Using the format of conferences and conventions, tens of thousands of people were reached with the message of the fullness of Christ. Bible believing Christians on both sides of the Atlantic were deeply affected.

Other Leaders of the Movement

D.L. Moody played an important role in the Higher Life movement. Moody had experienced the enduement of power. He attributed the success of his evangelistic meetings to the Holy Spirit. His evangelistic meetings in England were potent. Thousands attended, and many gave their lives to Christ.

Moody's ministry in England was at its peak when Smith and Boardman came to preach the Higher Life. Moody gave their conferences his full support. Back in America, Moody's conference at Northfield, Massachusetts, became a center for Higher Life teaching. Andrew Murray, A.T. Pierson and other Keswick and Higher Life advocates preached there. Moody's successor, R.A. Torrey, preached the baptism of the Holy Spirit with great power.

No account of the Higher Life movement would be complete without reference to A.J. Gordon of Boston. This able Baptist pastor, author and educator was filled with the Spirit long after he entered the ministry. He made holiness and healing prominent parts of his message at his great church and at the school he founded (now Gordon-Conwell Seminary).

Wheaton (Illinois) College was alive with Higher Life teaching. Charles Blanchard, the long-time president, preached holiness and healing to the students. He was a frequent speaker in Higher Life conferences. Like other leaders of this movement, Blanchard was a man of faith and prayer. He left to the church a legacy of Spirit-filled pastors and missionaries who graduated from his college.

Even its detractors concede that the Higher Life movement impacted the Western world. It produced revival, missionary zeal, fruitful evangelism, personal godliness. This dynamic movement of the Holy Spirit did much to shape the evangelical church of the 20th century in North America.

The Power of Literature

Literature was a force in the rapid spread of Higher Life teaching. Boardman's *The Higher Christian Life* was very popular in North America. It sold over 100,000 copies in a short time in England.

The Christian's Secret of a Happy Life, by Hannah Whitall Smith stirred great interest in the Higher Life. Her books and her speaking tours took the Christian public by storm. As a layperson, she presented the Higher Life in a devotional style. *The Christian's Secret of a Happy Life* can still be found in the religious section of most bookstores.

Andrew Murray, a Dutch Reformed pastor in South Africa, became a leading voice of the Higher Life movement. Fourteen of his books are still in print. The works of F.B. Meyer, an English Baptist minister, remain popular. Hopkins, prominent in the British Keswick movement, wrote a classic, *The Law of Liberty in the Spiritual Life,* still read by many today.

The writings of Simpson on themes of holiness and healing were a major contribution to the literature of the movement. His books, too, continue in print and are widely read in our day.

Present-Day Remnants of the Movement

More than two centuries have passed since the holiness movement begun by John and Charles Wesley became full-blown. More than a century has passed since the Higher Life movement reached its zenith. Methodism, including its many offshoots, is still very evident. Some sectors of it are much more spiritually alive than others. Likewise, remnants of the Higher Life movement still exist.

The Keswick conferences, adhering essentially to their original message, have encircled the globe, bringing blessing to tens of thousands—possibly hundreds of thousands—of Christians.

In Germany and Switzerland, what became known as the "Fellowship Movement" still has a following. The writings of Stockmayer, Johannes Blumhardt, Samuel Zeller and others are kept in print. In some cities interdenominational meetings teach the Higher Life to interested Christians.

Only one church denomination came out of the Higher Life movement. That was The Christian and Missionary Alliance. Simpson, its founder, and many of those associated with him had been influenced by the holiness movement and were committed to its general tenets. As The Christian and Missionary Alliance formed its doctrinal position, it made the fullness of Christ its distinctive message to the world.

Simpson and his associates were convinced that to carry out Christ's Great Commission, the church must be both pure and Spirit-empowered. From the

Higher Life perspective, holiness called for selfless service to Jesus Christ. The evidence of the Spirit's filling was not any specific gift but Christ-like character.

Conclusion

While somewhat weakened by the church's spiritual decline and drastic cultural changes in Western society, the teaching of scriptural holiness still appeals to Christians today. As the church of Jesus Christ approaches the threshold of the 21st century, it would do well to reexamine the history and literature of this 18th and 19th century visitation of the Holy Spirit.

The moral and spiritual weaknesses of the church in our time will only yield to full salvation in Christ. For the past two decades evangelical pastors in their preaching of the gospel have gone little beyond the message of forgiveness. As the French Protestant F. Godet said, "They seem to have no suspicion that salvation consists in the health of the soul, and that the health of the soul consists in holiness. Forgiveness is not the reestablishment of health, it is the crisis of convalescence. If God thinks fit to declare the sinner righteous, it is in order that He may by that means restore him to holiness."

It is time to raise the banner of Christ our Sanctifier and, on the simple terms of the Scriptures, urge God's people to meet Him in this blessed office. The indwelling of the God of holiness is the key to our spiritual health and wholeness.

CHAPTER 5

Holiness: the Doctrine

by Gerald E. McGraw

NAME YOUR TOP PRIORITY IN life. What pops into your mind? If you are young, finding a good wife or husband may head the list. If you are just getting started in a business or profession, success may be your number one priority. Or you might name happiness as your highest goal.

God advises, "Make every effort . . . to be holy; without holiness no one will see the Lord" (Hebrews 12:14). Here is a very solemn admonition. It implies that holiness should be your chief objective, *the top priority of your life.*

Don't let that word *doctrine* in the title of this chapter turn you off. Doctrine simply refers to teaching. It may be a collection of teachings (for example, Christian doctrine). It may be teaching on a single subject (the doctrine of sin, or the doctrine of salvation). The Christian church properly finds the heart of its teaching or doctrine in the Bible, God's infallible revelation to us.

If you've done much reading in the New Testament Letters, you know that the inspired writers invariably made their teaching practical. Theory (doctrine, teaching) is necessary, but it needs to be complemented by our day-to-day living.

When it comes to the doctrine of holiness, few sections of the Bible quite so ably combine doctrine and practice as Hebrews 12. That is where we will concentrate in this study.

Holiness Applies in Three Directions

Holiness describes right living in three directions: within ourselves, toward others and, supremely, toward God.

Place your hand on your chest. This gesture suggests that fulfilling God's command for holiness applies to *you yourself.* Think of holiness as starting with you because God has already laid all the necessary foundations.

God's Word impels us to make holiness an earnest pursuit. "Make every effort . . ." (NIV). "Pursue . . ." (NKJV, NRSV). As a cat relentlessly chases a mouse, as a hunter concentrates on the deer he is stalking, as a runner shuns every distraction in her race for the goal, so we are to pursue holiness. It must involve our desire, our attention, our effort, our endurance.

Extend your hand outward. It will help remind you of the second direction of holiness. Holiness closely concerns our attitudes, acts and words to *others.* We have relationships with other people, and holiness should display its sweet fragrance throughout those relationships.

The same verse that commands us to "make every effort . . . to be holy" says also, "Make every effort to live in peace with all men" (12:14). In contemporary society, strife rather than peace seems to mark the way people, families, committees and nations gain their advantage. Even enthusiasts upholding Christian moral causes often show fierce anger and hatred. God's holy people are to endeavor to live in peace with all others.

Now, will you reach your hand upward? The third direction of holiness is toward *God Himself.* He is everywhere—all around us and inside us who are His children. But I am suggesting you reach up because Jesus taught us to pray to "our Father in heaven" (Matthew 6:9).

Holiness reaches within ourselves, out to others and up to God.

Three Aspects of Holiness

The Scriptures speak of holiness in several aspects. What theologians have come to call *positional holiness* refers to our standing when we receive Jesus into our lives at conversion. The Bible describes even new or immature believers as "saints" (holy ones) (see, for example, 1 Corinthians 1:2, KJV). Calling us to Himself, making us new creations in Christ (2 Corinthians 5:17), God requires each of us to live the part as saints.

A second aspect of holiness marks the point at which the Christian, identifying with Christ in His death and resurrection, makes a full dedication of himself or herself to the Lord (Romans 6:11, 13). By faith he or she claims the filling of the Holy Spirit (Ephesians 5:18). Many believers have discovered this well-kept secret as the difference between mediocrity and a successful, empowered, Christ-centered life. Every hungry Christian should find this point. We use terms such as "filled with the Spirit" or "sanctified" or "the deeper life" to describe this important transaction between the believer and God. It's a *dynamic point holiness,* a *punctiliar holiness,* meaning we enter into this experience at a definite point of time.

Still a third aspect of holiness is what theologians refer to as *progressive holiness*—growth in Christ-likeness. Neither at salvation nor at sanctification have we fully arrived. God expects us to progress in holiness. Hebrews 12:14 uses a verb tense suggesting an ongoing effort to live this holy life. Thus the main thrust here seems to be the need to make progress. The imagery of the runner running a race (12:1) bears out this idea. Earlier, too, the writer has warned against retrogression. The surest way to avoid retreating is to advance!

Progressive holiness should not be understood as a good-works kind of righteousness. It rests on faith, even as do positional and dynamic point holiness. The holiness that all believers ought continually to strive to produce and to demonstrate can come only through the motivation and energy of the indwelling Christ.

Three Elements

In describing this holiness or purity before God, the Bible repeatedly speaks of three elements. All three have some relation to conversion, but more particularly they form a central core of experience when a person is sanctified. The sanctified Christian finds the same three elements highly significant in progressive holiness.

The first is *separation.* To run the race effectively,

a Christian must "hurl aside every encumbrance" (12:1 NASB). Runners when they race do not dress like astronauts. A long-distance runner's total outfit—shirt, shorts, shoes—weighs one pound! The runner separates himself or herself from all extra weight.

At conversion we dropped the sins on which Christ put His finger. In entering the sanctified, deeper life, we agree to separate ourselves from the self-life. Now, as we run to win, items that before seemed important will become dispensable. Winning costs something.

The second major element is *dedication*. We must regard ourselves as completely the Lord's. We gave our hearts to Him at conversion. We presented ourselves to Him without reserve when we entered into the deeper life. Now as we travel this highway of holiness, God expects us to live a continually dedicated life.

"We have all had human fathers who disciplined us and we respected them for it. How much more should we submit to the Father of our spirits and live!" (12:9). God wants all our desires, all our will, all of us.

The third element is *habitation*. At conversion we invited Jesus in. At the deeper life turning point, we make every part of our life available to His occupancy. In progressive holiness, we trust Christ to live out His own life unhindered through our yielded personality. We keep asking the Master to produce in and through us the holiness that He expects.

Do troubles and trials come? "God disciplines us for our good, that we may share in his holiness" (12:10).

Holiness Relates to Service

Holiness must relate to service. The godly person's right standing with God and growth in holiness concern not only purity but also power for service. "Let us show gratitude, by which we may offer to God an acceptable service with reverence and awe" (12:28, NASB). This service constitutes a New Covenant sacrifice on the altar to God. Our service supersedes the Old Testament animal sacrifices. It is an offering that God gladly accepts.

Often in our inertia and powerlessness, we need a fresh infilling with the Holy Spirit to do God's work. We ought to seek Him for the power so necessary to lead sinners to Christ and to lead Christians to holiness. Only He can do this through us. We need His power—whether to do mighty exploits or to complete menial tasks in everyday experience.

Progressive holiness underlies the performance of God's commands. Christendom in this postmodern era treats God's commands as though they were suggestions. God becomes the servant; *we* become lords. At Sinai Israel pledged obedience but quickly turned aside. God warns about the perils of disobedience:

> *See to it that you do not refuse him who speaks. If they did not escape when they refused him who warned them on earth, how much less will we, if we turn away from him who warns us from heaven?* (12:25)

Obedience furthers our growth in holiness. Disobedience stunts growth. He who requires our obedience deserves our obedience. "If you love me," Christ told His disciples, "you will obey what I command" (John 14:15). Will we, like Israel of old, turn aside to disobedience? If so, how shall we escape?

Hindrances to Holiness

Satan tries in every way possible to keep us from living a consistent life of progressive holiness. Sometimes he gets help from an unexpected source: us! We can be both target and enemy.

The internal enemy is what God calls sin. When the Scriptures use that word in the singular, it often refers to the sin principle within us. The Bible elsewhere names it "the flesh" or "self."

Self entangles us very easily (see Hebrews 12:1). Like with a fishing line, the tangles are much easier to get than to get out of. The writer to the Hebrews warns us of "the sin that so easily entangles."

Another difficulty within us is the tendency to want to give up. "See to it that no one misses [or forfeits, comes short of, fails to respond to] the grace of God" (12:15). When we become discouraged amid trials, we tragically miss God's provided grace and victory. It is very important in attaining and maintaining a holy life that we refuse to give up.

There is also the "bitter root" that "grows up to cause trouble and defile many" (12:15). Other people can affect us negatively. Likewise, we can derail others. All of us have experienced those times of feeling belittled, degraded, offended or even abused. We must deal decisively with life's hurts. Even as weeds can easily take over a garden, so bitter feelings can quickly dominate our lives. Sometimes Christians share life's hurts in such a way that the bitterness they harbor pollutes many others as well.

A Profane Person

The phrase that introduces the next hindrance to holiness in Hebrews 12 singles out Esau as "a fornicator or profane person" (12:16 KJV). Although Esau had married outside the chosen clan, the Old Testament never charges Jacob's twin with immorality. We probably should understand the writer here to be using the term figuratively (as the Scriptures often do). James, for example, says, "You adulterous people, don't you know that friendship with the world is hatred toward God?" (James 4:4). God treats our friendship with the world system as spiritual adultery, a violation of the covenant with our true Lover.

Esau's trespass consisted of a foolish life choice. That decision scorned the value of spiritual leadership within the family as well as certain material benefits. His offense was equivalent to saying, "This one meal is more important to me than my inheritance rights."

It is all too easy to make foolish big choices in life, to allow comparatively trivial concerns to change the course of our lives. We must avoid putting anything in the place of God. When we do, we have committed spiritual adultery.

Holiness Is Centered in a Person

Progressive holiness is centered in a person—the

Lord Jesus Christ. Pointing Jesus out as an example, the author challenges his readers, "Consider him" (12:3). This consideration should lead us to concentration and contemplation: "Let us fix our eyes on Jesus, the author and perfecter of our faith" (12:2). He who makes faith possible will also bring it to completion.

The word *fix* suggests looking away from other things to focus particularly on the object, in this case, Jesus. Glancing at the spectators can turn an athlete's attention away from the goal. Focusing on our own troubles can divert our attention from Christ Jesus.

Beyond serving as a model for us, Jesus by His death purchased our holiness. We behold Him "lifted up"—on the cross, suffering as He shed His blood to make us holy (12:2; 13:12). The Father exalted Him higher. Having risen from the grave, Jesus ascended to heaven. He "sat down at the right hand of the throne of God" (12:2). He poured out the empowering Spirit on the early church (Acts 2:33). Yet today this same *Holy* Spirit ministers to make believers more and more holy.

Jesus exchanged covenants for us (12:24). The old covenant, established at Mount Sinai, evoked dread and fear. It featured commandments written on stone, largely expressed in negative language: "You shall not . . ." "You shall not . . ." (see Exodus 20:3-17).

By contrast, positive language predominates in the New Covenant. The New Covenant supplies believers the power to obey those Old Covenant commandments (see Jeremiah 31:33-34) and writes them inside human hearts. In the sanctification process, God cleanses our desires so that we accomplish His will because we want to do so. His will becomes second nature. This great exchange figures prominently in our holiness.

Holiness Prepares Us for Heaven

Consider all the ways holiness prepares us for a glorious future in the hereafter. We "have not come to a mountain that can be touched and that is burning with fire; to darkness, gloom and storm; to a trumpet blast or to such a voice speaking words that those who heard it begged that no further word be spoken" (12:18-19). That, of course, is a reference to Mount Sinai.

Instead, we "have come to Mount Zion, to the heavenly Jerusalem, the city of the living God. . . . To thousands upon thousands of angels in joyful assembly, to the church of the firstborn, whose names are written in heaven. . . . To God, the judge of all men, to the spirits of righteous men made perfect, to Jesus the mediator of a new covenant, and to the sprinkled blood that speaks a better word than the blood of Abel" (12:22-24).

We have come to a holy city, to holy angels, to a holy church, to a holy Creator God, to a holy Jesus and to His holy cleansing blood. Moreover, it will be a holy commonwealth—the unshakable kingdom of God. *That is the kingdom we shall be receiving* (12:28).

Everything in that new order is holy. Can we ourselves expect to be the exception?

Summary

Holiness involves right-living—within ourselves, toward others and supremely toward God. No

61

doctrine is more practical.

Holiness centers on the person of Jesus, who Himself exhibited holiness, who purchased it for us through His atoning work, who makes it effective in our lives. Everything having to do with our eternal hope is holy. Holiness helps us for the present and prepares us for the imminent future.

Are you holy now? Are you more holy than you were six months ago? Only as you now are living in progressive holiness are you properly preparing for the holy city that is coming.

The habit of implicit obedience, the recognition of God's absolute authority, and the recognition of all His commands as sacred constitute the very groundwork of a holy life. God conditioned victory for Joshua on his obedience: "Be careful to obey all the law my servant Moses gave you; do not turn from it to the right or to the left, that you may be successful wherever you go" (Joshua 1:7).
—A.B. Simpson—

Holiness, the Unarticulated Yearning

by Thomas B. Kyle

FOR A DECADE OR MORE, the integrity of the church in North America has been plummeting. The sins of some of its most visible representatives are the tip of an iceberg that involves a large cross section of church members and church goers.

Indifference has become an accepted attitude. We are surrounded by material advantage. Life is full to the brim. And God? Well, He gets a part of our lives, but certainly not all.

With little time for God, we do little growing in Christ. There may be little difference between the "before" and "after" pictures that we present. We do not include God in our lives on His terms, and we hope He won't mind. We have attempted to fashion the sovereign God into a god who can't change anything, challenge anyone or command our attention.

There is a deadly notion in many quarters that God doesn't expect as much of us today as He expected of past generations. Possibly we can take back some of our commitment, regain partial control of our lives. God can still use us—we're not opposed to that—but He will have to lower His expectations somewhat.

The deteriorating moral climate within our North American culture has not helped. People are consulting with "angelic beings" and paying several dollars a minute to talk with psychics who know it all. Spiritism has come to North America big-time.

A Yearning for Something More

The good news amid such a doleful picture is what I see as a growing concern among many of God's people for something more, for a life-style that reflects Christlike virtues and values.

As I travel the length and breadth of the continent in evangelistic campaigns, I sense a yearning among the community of believers for a fresh visitation from God. A growing number of people are convinced that the time for repentance, renewal and a return to righteousness is at hand. It is time for all of us in the household of faith to "clean up our act," live lives pleasing to God and be true overcomers.

During my missionary service in Brazil, one of my responsibilities was to help develop Hallelujah Valley, a Christian camp about thirty miles from Curitiba, Parana. When I arrived, there was a swimming pool completed except for the deepest part of the concrete floor.

There the mud was deep and thick. Decaying debris caused it to smell like rotten eggs. Snakes and crabs nipped at our boots. But right in the midst of all that decay and stench and filth that we were digging out was a spring of crystal-clear, cold water, pure enough to drink.

That describes our potential as Christians. We are

surrounded by the rot of human logic, by the sludge of political correctness that demeans God. In such an environment God makes available to us the power to be pure and clean, to say by word and deed that Jesus Christ can make a difference.

Only on God's Terms

We can only experience God's qualities of "love, joy, peace, patience, kindness, goodness, faithfulness, gentleness and self-control" (Galatians 5:22-23) on God's terms. There is no single injection of perfection, no once-only shot of holiness that will suffice for the rest of our lives. Holy living must be a life-style. It is what we are in Christ. It is Christ in us.

The biblical command, "Do not get drunk on wine" (Ephesians 5:18) speaks of the spirits in the bottle, but it applies as well to the various spirits and ideologies of our age, the effect of which can be as intoxicating. On the other hand, the second part of the command—"Instead, be filled with the Spirit"—promises to be a continuous spring of purity, peace, power and purpose in our lives.

The "how" of this renewal experience need not be a deep mystery. The Scriptures offer us clear guidance.

Parents who have found it necessary to leave children at home for a few days with a guardian while they traveled remember the endless lists of instructions they prepared: phone numbers where they could be reached, a list of things to be done, the time to get up and go to bed, chores to do—the list was infinite. They read the instructions to themselves to make sure they had forgotten nothing, then to the kids, finally to the one they were leaving in charge. Five miles down the road, they were still wondering if their instructions were clear and complete.

In John 14-16 we have the "instruction list" that Jesus gave His disciples as He prepared to leave earth for heaven. "I am going away to prepare a place for you, but don't worry, I will never leave you alone. Here is how we will stay in touch: I will send you a Helper and He will guide you. In case of problems or if you forget what I have told you, this Helper will be there."

Instructions to Keep in Mind

As in most farewells, people are overtaken by the emotion of the moment and the last-minute goodbyes. They forget some of the important things. That is the whole reason for writing down the instructions—to review them later so as to be able to carry out all the wishes of the person or persons who made up the list. The disciples would slip, deny, hide, have momentary lapses of memory, but eventually what the Master had taught them would burst forth in their living and language.

We will never understand the Holy Spirit until we have read and mastered John 14-16. In those chapters Jesus articulates for us the *Who* of renewal and holy living. It is our list of instructions about the Holy Spirit and what we are to do.

We read there that the Holy Spirit will come to "convict the world of guilt in regard to sin and righteousness and judgment" (John 16:8). We have a tendency to forget lostness. Our prayer for renewal and holiness must also include a prayer of repentance for neglecting our part in winning people to Christ.

Conviction of sin produces repentance. When that occurs, God begins to communicate with us in our spirits that we are His children (Romans 8:16). As we listen to His voice, the Holy Spirit confirms to us that we are part of the body of Christ (1 Corinthians 12:13). What a comfort to know that we have been brought into the family of God!

Jesus also declared that it was to the disciples' advantage that He should go away. By leaving, He could send the Holy Spirit to take His place, and the Holy Spirit would "guide [them] into all truth" (John 16:13). We need to realize that the Spirit came to fulfill Christ's mission on earth. Jesus said, "He will bring glory to me by taking from what is mine and making it known to you" (16:14).

A Messenger of Truth

The various themes proposed by politicians and moral pundits simply substitute human logic and human codes of rightness for God's. Society is really saying, "We can handle it ourselves." We want a fair, honest, loving person, but we want such a person without God in the picture. We want what God represents, but we do not want God.

The Holy Spirit comes to represent Jesus Christ in our person, to live Christ through us in our actions and words. He came to stamp Christ in us from the inside out. Jesus said the Holy Spirit would guide us into all truth and make us truthful.

My father was always upset—justifiably so—when one of his children lied to him. When it happened, we could expect to be punished. After I became a

Christian it was also my heavenly Father who was grieved when I was not truthful. I soon realized that He would not tolerate so shallow a life. He is truth (John 14:6), and He will guide and teach us in truth.

We live in the age of easy access to information (not all of it necessarily truth). There are computers, satellites, faxes, fiber optics, phones in your pocket, beepers on your belt. The world has its voices of propaganda trying to fill our minds with its viewpoints. Buses often look like moving billboards. The landscape along our highways details the advantages of stopping at certain destinations. Symbols quickly digested into our minds speed us along our cement corridors. Bumper stickers continue to hold their own on this superhighway of information.

"Honk if you love Jesus" was plastered to the nicked-up bumper just in front of us one summer evening as we inched our way to the ticket booth at the Minneapolis/St. Paul Airport parking exit. I was just about to hit the horn button when to my surprise the voice I heard from inside the car ahead did not agree with the slogan on the bumper. The tones were angry, the language was vulgar. There had been a collision of cultures. Language and the way we use it says more about our level of Spirit-control than any other test we face.

In God's Image

Maurice is one of the most dignified persons I have ever known. Blue suit, white shirt, proper tie. Impeccable, even to the bald spot in the center of the back of his head.

I was returning to Brazil following ministry in the United States. The flight from São Paulo to Curitiba would be—as usual—late. Airports, in my experience, offer no good options for the average traveler who must wait. Either you choose to eat overpriced food, or you sit on molded plastic seats so uncomfortable you soon stand, or you pace the corridors. I chose to pace.

And there ahead of me was Maurice. I was *certain* it was my friend—even to the bald spot in the center of the back of his head. But when I spoke and he turned around, I realized I had made a mistake. The similarities were uncanny: same type of suit, shirt, shoes, manner of walking. Even the cadence in his voice as he spoke reminded me of Maurice.

I soon discovered why. This man was Maurice, Senior. I knew his son, Maurice, Junior. And because of that, I also knew something of his father.

The Holy Spirit wants to fill us with the person of Christ so that His purity, His personality, His power will transform us from the inside out. Words like real, honest, authentic, forgiving, loving, gracious, considerate will begin to describe our lives as He invades us. The similarities will be so great we will begin to look like, sound like, walk like "Christones."

A Clear Message

God's message to us is clear: "I urge you, . . . in view of God's mercy, to offer your bodies as living sacrifices, holy and pleasing to God" (Romans 12:1). Our part is to present ourselves to God, to pursue Him each day. As many pursue physical fitness, so our spiritual pursuit must be daily. The difficulty is in taking time to let it happen.

If you don't have the good habit of daily devotions, make a start with five Bible verses, well-read and meditated on. Then take five minutes to talk with God about your needs. Present yourself to Him. Talk to Him about the things that need fixing in your life. Fill your mind with new images and thoughts from the Scriptures. An idle mind is fertile ground for all types of polluted thoughts. Fill your mind with good books, godly conversation, great music and positive thoughts.

Suppose you were to be an overnight guest of ours. And suppose when it came bedtime my wife or I would say, "We're glad you are here. We want you to be comfortable, but would you mind sleeping by the entry door tonight? We don't want you creating any inconvenience for us by using an upstairs bedroom. Here's a blanket and a pillow." And with that we would be off upstairs to bed.

You probably wouldn't sleep very much. You would be on the inside, but just barely. You would stay dry if it rained, warm if it turned cold, but with the rest of the house off limits to you, it wouldn't be much of a stay. We allowed you the least possible amount of space.

Many treat the Holy Spirit just that way. They crowd Him into the least space possible. Basically they ignore Him. They have never taken Him to the attic where so much remains to be sorted out. Or to the cellar, where all the clutter of the old life remnants, lying in the dim light of self-rule, need to be tossed out. Neither do they allow Him on the main floor where decisions are made and life is lived.

Jesus says the Holy Spirit will be given to those who ask. "If you then . . . know how to give good gifts to your children, how much more will your Father in heaven give the Holy Spirit to those who ask him!" (Luke 11:13). The asking is walking Him through our lives, permitting Him to occupy every place within us.

Simply Ask

We must ask the Holy Spirit to fill us with Himself and the qualities of Christ so that we will desire to please God in every aspect of our lives. Over the years I have used this prayer for myself and in public services. I share it with you:

> *Almighty God,*
> *I come to You in the name of the Lord Jesus Christ. I do believe with all my heart that Jesus has been raised from the dead to be my salvation, to be my justification, to be my sanctification.*
> *I now take a firm stand against sin in my life and against sin's power in my spirit, soul and body. I resist it, renounce it and refuse it in all of its forms. In the name of Jesus Christ and through His shed blood, I now bind and break the complete powers of evil in or against me from any source.*
> *I acknowledge that I have been directing my own life. In this I have sinned against You. I ask Your forgiveness. I take a stand against self. By faith I put it to death with all its affections, and I count myself dead to sin.*
> *Teach me, O Lord, through Your Word. Help me to cultivate the desire to know You. I do desire to be a Spirit-filled Christian.*
> *By faith I reach out to You now and ask to be filled with the Holy Spirit. I invite You to live in*

every part of my person.

Renew, I pray, my mind. Plant in the soil of my soul the seed of the fruit of the Spirit: "love, joy, peace, patience, kindness, goodness, faithfulness, gentleness and self-control" (Galatians 5:22-23).

I do by faith choose to live and walk in the Spirit. Place in me a new power to witness. Help me to set my affections to serve You in true holiness and righteousness.

For Christ's sake, Amen.

"Yes, Lord"

The year was 1957. It was the Fourth of July weekend. The weather was hot and muggy. Minnesota mosquitoes were out in full force. That's when I married Mary.

There was no air-conditioning in the little church, filled with friends and relatives. The music rang out, and there I stood at the altar in my too-tight rented attire, my soon-to-be bride beside me. The burning candles, the churchful of perspiring bodies, the stifling day, the lack of ventilation were just too much. I passed out at my wedding!

My brother, Jim, best man, held me up on one side and my wife-to-be did her best to hang on until it was official. At the right moment I managed to mutter "Yes." The minister pronounced us man and wife, we kissed each other and made a safe passage up the aisle to the door and to fresh air.

If you have a license, witnesses and the proper official, that little word *Yes* is all it takes to get you married. The same word will keep your marriage working. If you are into difficulties in your marriage, the best way to get back to what got it all going is another "Yes." Yes, I'll wait for you to finish your shopping. Yes, I'll carry out the garbage. Yes, I love you. Yes!

When we came to Christ, no matter what the words were that we prayed, we said, "Yes, Lord, be my Savior!" *Yes* got the transaction going. We passed from death to life. We were born again. It is so simple that many miss it.

Yes brings the Holy Spirit into your life in His fullness. "Yes, Lord, I count myself dead to sin. Yes, Lord, I hand everything over to You." And *Yes, Lord,* will keep the experience alive and fresh.

Over and over the Holy Spirit will articulate to us the things of Christ. Our response must always be an unreserved "Yes, Lord."

The divine order is first reconciliation, then godliness. Not only are we brought near to God through the blood of Christ, but through Him we can walk in His commandments. We who have been redeemed at such cost and brought into this place of privilege, are to be holy even as God is holy.
—A.B. Simpson—

| CHAPTER 7 | Holiness and the Cross |

by Robert B. Goldenberg

HOLINESS BEGINS AT THE CROSS of Jesus Christ. It begins with a dying to self. It is not a very popular viewpoint, as I have discovered in my ten years of pastoral ministry.

Like most pastors, I have suffered the pain of losing friends who did not like what I preached. I must admit it has been a major source of frustration for me. They listened as I preached holiness by way of the cross and death to self. Now they sit in more comfortable pews down the road.

In one sense I cannot blame them. Why continue to listen to a message that calls for death to self when they can hear a message of blessing, blessing and more blessing? Why listen to a message about a Savior who said, "Take up your cross and follow Me," when they can join in a seemingly cross-less Christianity involving little or no sacrifice?

"Me First" Is Still Alive and Well

Let's face it. We may live in a post me-generation, but the Take-Care-of-Number-One philosophy is still alive and well. Let's also face the fact that this message has found its way into the pulpits of many North American churches. If you don't believe it, check out the ratio of per capita missionary dollars to per capita income now with what it was a century ago. The church does not want to hear about giving, about sacrifice, about doing without. Christians, like the others, want to have it all now, but they don't want to pay for it until much later.

This makes a message about holiness and the cross difficult to preach. I suspect it is more difficult to preach it today than ever before. But until the church learns that true holiness starts at the foot of the cross of Christ, we will continue to miss the opportunity for real depth and strength in our relationship with God.

It is not a fun-and-games message, this message of the cross. It will never tickle the ears of most listeners. It will not attract large crowds. People do not want to hear about death to self. They do not want to learn about a personal cross. That is why so many preachers have watered down the message, hoping for something more palatable.

The message of holiness has gone from Jesus' call to take up the cross to man's call to put on the divine Dove. Sanctification, which began as a message about surrendering to God, has become a shopping list of what we want from God. This has affected other parts of church life also. Worship has become a time to be entertained. Prayer is an occasion to draw attention to oneself. The offering has turned into a bribe to get from God more than we give.

It ought not to be that way. The church is the only place in the world where a real message of holiness can be presented. Christians are the only people in the world who can hear this message with any hope of assimilating it into their lives.

Holiness Defined

Let me attempt to define holiness. Although it involves morality, it does not mean being moral. Every civilized person, Christian and non-Christian, should be moral. Immorality should have no place in an orderly society.

Although holiness involves being ethical, holiness is not about being ethical. Doing the right and proper thing is the responsibility of us all. Most people, with or without Christ, know the difference between right and wrong.

In fact, holiness is not an action at all. It is a state of being. Granted we should be able to see the difference between a holy life and an unholy life. But we are looking at a result, not an action. Holiness will lead to moral and ethical living, but moral and ethical living will not lead to holiness.

Holiness is being sold out *to*—not *for*—Jesus. Holy people have died to self-interest and even self-preservation. They have given themselves over to God. No longer do they concern themselves with their own needs. Their only concern is what God wants.

This is not a place for the unconverted. Those who have not entrusted God with their eternal destiny can hardly be expected to entrust Him with their lives now. But as impossible as this is for the non-Christian, it is far from easy even for the Christian. The fact is, it is tough to die to self. We are, after all, self-centered and self-protective people.

Holiness Must Start at the Cross

That brings us back to my thesis: *Holiness must start at the cross.* That may seem like a simple enough statement. But even the few Christians who genuinely desire true holiness do not want to begin their journey at the cross. Somewhere, anywhere— but not at the cross.

People prefer to begin from the lap of God. Like little children, we see ourselves climbing into the lap of a giant, heavenly Vending Machine. We put in our nickels and dimes and expect blessing in return. We have reduced holiness to a series of "gimmies"—"Gimme blessings," "Gimme power," "Gimme the Holy Spirit so I can be a bigger, better, flashier Christian." Dying to self has no place in this "gimme" view of sanctification.

One of the problems with such a twisted theology of holiness is that we never have to get empty before we get filled. We want to indulge in the things of God, but there is no room. We are too full of the things of self. Our motives may be good. We want to serve God better. We want to be better witnesses. We want the power of God flowing through our lives. Most of the time it's not our motives that need to change, but our direction.

So Right and Yet So Wrong

It all sounds so spiritual! "All I want is power to witness, the blessings due my children, the tools to live closer to God." It is amazing how things so right can be twisted into something so wrong.

Power to witness has become a spotlight pointing to the messenger rather than the message. God almost becomes an instrument in the whole thing. "Make my ministry bigger!" The crowds take notice not of the God who is supposed to be touching people's lives but of the minister who should be pointing the way. We add notches to the bindings of our Bibles for every "soul" won and duly report the total to headquarters and to our supporters.

Somehow the bread due the children has been turned into steak. The children of the King have forgotten that the wedding banquet does not happen until the Bridegroom returns. Who-is-the-most-blest? has become a contest played out in churches across the continent.

For the most part, the name-it-and-claim-it theology of the past decade has died. But it left some baggage behind. There is still the erroneous belief that the person not given much must not be where God wants him or her to be. "The one with the most blessings must be closest to God."

Even something as wonderful as the gifts of the Spirit can be turned to glorify the receiver more than the Giver. Like Joseph, showing off his coat of many colors, some go around using (read that *showing off*) their gifts as if to say, "The Father loves me more than He loves you."

Getting More or Wanting Less?

I often wonder how we in North America must look to many of our brothers and sisters in the Third World—in places where Jesus is preached and embraced amid abject poverty, in places where Christians understand what it really means to "be content whatever the circumstances" (Philippians 4:11). And, more often than not, the circumstances

78

are not good. Does being holy mean getting more? Or could it mean wanting less?

In our twisted view of holiness we picture Christians opening themselves up and receiving something from God—sort of like walking down the road of life and the Holy Spirit comes in the form of a dove and lands on them like He did on Jesus. We do not "add" holiness like we would a diamond-studded "Jesus" brooch.

Jesus made it clear that the journey to a holy life, set apart to God, does not begin with good motives. It begins by focusing only on God and wanting only what He wants. It does not start in the amusement park of self-excess—"Fill me," "Bless me." It starts in the Garden of Gethsemane where we die to what we want and declare to God, "Not my will, but Yours." It starts by accepting the fact that if we never get blessed, never feel the power, never know the highs, it's all right because God is in complete control. In fact, letting God be in control is the key in this process.

It is not much fun. Death never is. Maybe that's why Jesus said "Take up your cross" rather than "Take up your picnic basket." That's why He spoke about losing your life rather than filling your life. No, it is not much fun. In fact, it can be downright painful. Sometimes we—read that *I*—want to avoid it at all costs. But, nonetheless, it is the holy life God has called us to.

Like Salvation

Holiness begins at the cross of Jesus Christ. That's where salvation began—at the same cross and in a similar struggle. When we became Christians, we knew there were things we had to give up. We knew we needed help. For some of us it was a long, hard struggle to admit that what we needed was a Savior to come to our rescue.

At some point in the salvation experience, we had to die to ourselves and accept God's provision in Christ Jesus. The problem for some born-again Christians is that the death was short-lived. Very quickly they learned again how to be self-sufficient. It was easy to leave the cross and once again stand on their own two feet without God's help. Or so they thought.

Holiness is a trip back to that same cross from which we started. Holiness is a trip back to the Garden and to Golgotha.

When Paul wrote, "I want to know Christ and the power of his resurrection and the fellowship of sharing in his sufferings, becoming like him in his death" (Philippians 3:10), he was giving us the essence of holiness.

What did he mean when he said he wanted to be like Christ in His death? Did he mean he wanted to go to Calvary and physically die on a cross? I don't think that was his point. Paul wanted to die to his self-will just as Christ had "died" in the Garden. Paul knew that true holiness comes at the cost of our self-desire.

Death to self is also what Jesus was speaking about when He said to those who were following Him, "If anyone would come after me, he must deny himself and take up his cross daily and follow me. For whoever wants to save his life will lose it, but whoever loses his life for me will save it" (Luke 9:23-24).

We Will Never Be Self-Sufficient

Another part of the self life that must die is self-sufficiency. To suppose that we have what we need to live the Christian life flies directly in the face of the Scriptures. In Philippians 3 Paul recalls his own impeccable pedigree and quickly adds, "Whatever was to my profit I now consider loss for the sake of Christ" (3:7). Paul had nothing to offer in his own standing with God.

Jesus and Paul taught a truth that we desperately need to learn afresh today. Real holiness comes at the cost of self. That real holiness is not about gifts and talents. It's not about blessing and power. It is about surrender. Real holiness is achieved when we pick up our own personal cross and allow God to crucify our flesh, our wants, our desires on it. It is not fun. Death never is. But real holiness—holiness that starts at the cross—brings with it a richness like nothing else.

There is no peace like the peace that comes with genuine holiness. When we can stand up and proclaim with absolute assurance that there is nothing negative between us and God—at that point we know real peace. Like the calm following physical death, there is a calm that follows the death of self.

Jesus said, "If anyone would come after me, he must deny himself and take up his cross and follow me" (Matthew 16:24). He was serious. Holiness—a life totally surrendered to God—starts at the cross. It begins with self-death. It continues with the daily commitment to God's will and God's way.

Holiness, God's Expectation

by Arnold R. Fleagle

IF HOLINESS IS GOD'S EXPECTATION, the church of Jesus Christ is drifting! No less an observer than J.I. Packer concedes as much. "I see sanctification as a neglected priority in today's church everywhere," Packer writes, "and a fading glory in the evangelical church in particular."

Holy is what God expects His church to be. Hear what His Word has to say:

> *Therefore, prepare your minds for action; be self-controlled; set your hope fully on the grace to be given you when Jesus Christ is revealed. As obedient children, do not conform to the evil desires you had when you lived in ignorance. But just as he who called you is holy, so be holy in all you do; for it is written: "Be holy, because I am holy."* (1 Peter 1:13-16)

Holiness Is Our Obligation

Holiness is the Christian's obligation! Sanctification should be the norm! God challenges the church to be transported to the highlands of spiritual, moral and ethical triumph. He calls the church from the lowlands of spiritual mediocrity.

In *Idols for Destruction,* Herbert Schlossberg fires this painful assessment at the church: "Protestantism has largely divested itself of the transcendent and has become almost indistinguishable from the surrounding culture" (page 38). It is a sad commentary on the state of the church and its constituents.

The dynamic followers of Jesus Christ should be a *counterculture* to those who are living apart from God. They should manifest a *contrast,* not a conformity, to those who are lost. Instead, the distinction between those who are "in Christ" and those who are "outside of Christ" is not clear. Darkness and light have merged into a disappointing gray.

A.W. Tozer, in his inimitable style, puts it this way in *I Talk Back to the Devil:*

> *In many churches Christianity has been watered down until the solution is so weak that if it were poison it would not hurt anyone and if it were medicine it would not cure anyone! . . .*
>
> *Most modern Christians live sub-Christian lives! Most Christians are not joyful persons because they are not holy persons, and they are not holy persons because they are not filled with the Holy Spirit, and they are not filled with the Holy Spirit because they are not separated persons.*
>
> *The Spirit cannot fill whom He cannot separate, and whom He cannot fill He cannot make holy, and whom He cannot make holy He cannot make happy!* (page 36)

A Holiness Agenda

"Prepare your minds for action." The phrase conveyed a particular image to first-century Christians. William Barclay explains:

> In the east men wore long, flowing robes which hindered fast progress or strenuous action. Round the waist they wore a broad belt or girdle. When strenuous action was necessary, they shortened the long robe by pulling it up within the belt in order to give them freedom of movement. (The Letters of James and Peter, page 183)

In short, tuck in what will slow you down, and position yourself to run the race that God has designed for you.

"Be self-controlled." Another trait of a saved life is self-control. "Like a city whose walls are broken down / is a man who lacks self-control" (Proverbs 25:28). Self-control is listed in the fruit of the Spirit (Galatians 5:22-23). It is a requisite of elders in church leadership (1 Timothy 3:2). Peter will use it two other times in the short letter: "The end of all things is near. Therefore be clear minded and self-controlled so that you can pray" (1 Peter 4:7). "Be self-controlled and alert. Your enemy the devil prowls around like a roaring lion looking for someone to devour" (5:8).

The Spirit-filled Christian will reflect the residency of the divine nature. He or she will be governed by the core values of God's Word. Christian ethics and calm confidence will prevail. Rowland Hill contends, "I would give nothing for that man's religion whose very dog and cat are not the better for it." It was John Wesley who said, "Orthodoxy is at best a very slender part of religion." Along with orthodoxy (right opinion) there must be orthopraxis (straight living). That is the holiness expectation.

Look Ahead

"Set your hope fully on the grace to be given you when Jesus Christ is revealed." God's kingdom comes when Jesus Christ returns. He completes the benefit package of salvation.

This final denouement provides a compelling incentive to live a consistent and consecrated life of holiness! As Browning summed it up: "The best is yet to be." In the middle of frustrating days and long nights, the authentic believer can rest his or her weary head on that pillow of comfort: "The best is yet to be."

"As obedient children . . ." Peter employs the analogy of children, a recurring concept in the imagery of the redeemed in the New Testament, used also by Jesus, Paul and John. There are compliant children and there are defiant children. Peter is saying the former, not the latter, should distinguish God's sons and daughters.

These children are to be transformed by their faith and not conformed to the evil desires that occupied their pre-conversion pursuits. "Do not conform to the evil desires you had when you lived in ignorance."

"Do not conform" is a strong imperative. We contemporary Christians blend too easily into our environment. Again, Tozer expresses it graphically:

"We have reached a low place of sand and burnt wire grass . . . and accepted this low plane as the very pasture of the blessed" (page 107).

The people of God were to be distinguished from the society in which they lived. God's children were to be easily recognized for their adherence to God's Word, God's will and God's way!

A Crystal-Clear Call to Holiness

"But . . ." That contrary conjunction in 1:15 pivots the discussion to a crystal-clear call to holiness. God is holy! He is described as holy more often than He is described as loving or righteous or just. Holiness is God's primary attribute!

Exactly what do we mean by *holy*? It is a word that communicates contrast. Its basic root means "to set apart, to distinguish." It is often used to describe God, for He, above all else, is set apart from His creation—perfectly pure, without flaw.

In the New Testament, the Greek equivalent, *hagiazo*, can be found in 13 of the 27 books. It appears a total of 28 times, four of them in our text: "Just as he who called you is holy, so be holy in all you do; for it is written: 'Be holy, because I am holy.'"

The reference is to God's statement in Leviticus 11:44-45: "I am the LORD your God; consecrate yourselves and be holy, because I am holy. . . . I am the LORD who brought you up out of Egypt to be your God; therefore be holy, because I am holy."

Peter anchors the call to Christian holiness in the reality of God's holiness.

The implications are profound, as Jerry Bridges observes in *The Pursuit of Holiness*:

Because God is holy, He requires that we be holy. Many Christians have what we might call a "cultural holiness." They adapt to the character and behavior pattern of Christians around them. As the Christian culture around them is more or less holy, so these Christians are more or less holy. But God has not called us to be like those around us. He has called us to be like Himself. Holiness is nothing less than conformity to the character of God. (pages 25-26)

Wanted: Holy Men and Women

Where are the men and women whose morality reflects God's holiness, whose light shines in darkness, whose presence is an island of fragrance in a stench-filled room? Where are the men and women whose lives are a counterculture to the world's non-theistic ethic? As the apostles called first-century Christians to lives of holiness, so today's disciples of Christ are to put holiness on their daily agenda. Holiness is the drumbeat of the Christian of any age in any age.

Oswald Chambers issues the same call in a passage from *My Utmost for His Highest*:

> *Continually restate to yourself what the purpose of your life is. The destined end of an individual is not happiness, not health but holiness.*
>
> *The one thing that matters most is whether a person will accept the God who will make him holy. At all costs one must be rightly related to God. . . .*
>
> *God has one destined end for humans: holiness. He is not an eternal "blessing machine" for people.*

87

He did not come to save people out of pity. He came to save people because He had created them to be holy. (pages 403-404)

The manifestation of holiness by humanity cannot be synthetically produced. The holy life, or "sanctified life," must be implemented by the prevailing presence of the Holy Spirit. A.W. Tozer, in his small but significant booklet, *How to Be Filled with the Holy Spirit*, prescribes these steps:

How to Be Filled with the Holy Spirit

First, present your body to [God] (Romans 12:1-2). God can't fill what He can't have. Now I ask you: Are you ready to present your body with all its functions and all that it contains—your mind, your personality, your spirit, your love, your ambitions, your all? That is the first thing. That is a simple, easy act—presenting the body. Are you willing to do it?

Now the second thing is to ask (Luke 11:9-11), and I set aside all theological objections to this text. They say that it is not for today. Well, why then did the Lord leave it in the Bible? Why didn't He put it somewhere else? Why did He put it where I could see it if He didn't want me to believe it? It is all for us, and if the Lord wanted to, He could give {the Spirit} without our asking, but He chooses to have us ask. "Ask of me and I will give" is always God's order, so why not ask?

Acts 5:32 tells us the third thing to do. God gives His Holy Spirit to those who obey Him. Are you ready to obey and do what you are asked to do?

What would that be? Simply to live by the Scriptures as you understand them. Simple, but revolutionary.

The next thing is, have faith (Galatians 3:2). We receive [the Holy Spirit] by faith just as we received the Lord in salvation by faith. He comes as a gift of God to us in power. First He comes in some degree and measure when we are converted. Without Him we couldn't be born again, because we are born of the Spirit. But I am talking about something different now, an advance over that. I am talking about His coming and possessing the full body and mind and life and heart, taking over the whole personality, gently but directly and bluntly, and making it His, so that we may become a habitation of God through the Spirit. (pages 47-48)

When God's Priorities Become Ours

Let men and women pursue God, let them bring to Him open vessels to be filled, let them comprehend that God is the Potter and they are the clay, let them aim for the clouds and not the treetops, let them radiate holiness and display Christ-likeness. Then a renewal movement will sweep over our churches. And if enough churches join it, then a renewal movement will sweep over our communities. And if enough communities join in, then a renewal movement will sweep over our states and provinces, our nations, our continent.

Charles G. Finney, one of the giants in the history of American revivals, in his book *Crystal Christianity* had these words for 19th century believers:

One holy church crucified to the world would do more to promote Christianity than all the churches in the country, living as they do now. If I had strength to go through the churches, I would preach to bring them up to the standard of holy living. Of what use is it to convert sinners and make them such Christians as these? Of what use is it to try to convert sinners and make them feel that there is something in religion, and then by your conformity to the world prove there is nothing in it?

Where shall the Lord look for a church—like the first church—that will be separate and serve God? (page 159)

The holy heart is a burning heart. Elton Trueblood wrote a book about the church and entitled it, *The Incendiary Fellowship.* Indeed, the fire of God burns amid God's holy people. John Wesley once remarked, "Get on fire for God and people will come to see you burn!"

A burning bush attracted Moses' attention. In scaled down fashion, God's children are "burning bushes" in this world who call attention to God and a holy life-style made possible through Jesus Christ.

"Be holy because I am holy" was the divine expectation for the New Testament church. The passing of time has not eroded God's expectations for His children—holiness!

Holiness and the Fourfold Gospel

Salvation and Holiness

by Maurice R. Irvin

THERE IS AN OFT-TOLD AND probably apocryphal story of a European queen who looked out her palace window and saw her young son playing in a mud puddle.

"Get out of the mud!" she called to him. "Remember that you are a prince."

Whether or not the incident actually happened, in fact the Apostle Paul begins his first letter to the Christians at Corinth with very much that kind of an appeal. The believers at Corinth were in the mud. We learn from reading the entire letter that there were divisions in the church, there was immorality in their midst, believer was taking believer to court. Sacrilege had entered their observances of the Lord's Supper. The improper use of spiritual gifts had brought disorder to their worship services. Paul calls the Corinthian Christians "infants in Christ" and "worldly" (1 Corinthians 3:1).

Yet at the very beginning of his letter to them, the apostle describes their high standing through their relationship with Jesus. Indeed, he seems to be laying a groundwork for saying in all the rest of the epistle, "Get out of the mud! Remember that you are saints."

> Paul, called to be an apostle of Christ Jesus by the will of God, and our brother Sosthenes,
>
> To the church of God in Corinth, to those sanctified in Christ Jesus and called to be holy, together with all those everywhere who call on the name of our Lord Jesus Christ—their Lord and ours:
>
> Grace and peace to you from God our Father and the Lord Jesus Christ.
>
> I always thank God for you because of his grace given you in Christ Jesus. For in him you have been enriched in every way—in all your speaking and in all your knowledge—because our testimony about Christ was confirmed in you. Therefore you do not lack any spiritual gift as you eagerly wait for our Lord Jesus Christ to be revealed. He will keep you strong to the end, so that you will be blameless on the day of our Lord Jesus Christ. God, who has called you into fellowship with his Son Jesus Christ our Lord, is faithful. (1 Corinthians 1:1-9)

These verses, directed first to the Corinthians, present the same appeal and challenge to everyone of us Christians. Our very privileged standing provides an incentive and the enabling for us to get out of dirty puddles and to walk in cleanness and honor. We ought, then, to look very carefully at these opening verses of First Corinthians. And as we do, we discover here descriptions of *position*, *purpose* and *provisions*.

The Believer's *Position*

Right at the beginning, Paul declares that we Christians are sanctified in Christ Jesus. The word *sanctified* means set apart unto God. Paul's understanding of that term was shaped by Old Testament references to holy (sanctified) people, mountains, vessels, buildings (the tabernacle and temple) and days. In the Old Testament these things, taken from the realm of the common and ordinary, became God's particular possession to be used only for His purposes.

I looked one day at a dozen or more diamonds spread out in front of me on a velvet cloth. With a jeweler's help and advice, I selected one of the stones and had it set in a ring. From then until now, that diamond has been in the engagement ring my wife wears on her finger. I bought it and set it apart exclusively for Darolyn. In no less a sense, these Old Testament people, places and objects were set apart to belong to God alone—to be, as it were, diamonds in a ring on His finger.

In his salutation to the Corinthians Paul uses that great word *sanctified* to teach us that at the very moment we enter by faith into a vital relationship with Christ, we are removed from the realm of the ordinary, the commonplace. We now are God's particular possession, set apart for His purposes.

As Christians we have been brought out of the dominion of darkness (Colossians 1:13). We are no longer foreigners and aliens (Ephesians 2:19). We no longer belong to this world and its ways (Ephesians 2:1-2). We are no longer under the slavery of sin (Romans 6:6-7). Instead, we are chosen ones (1 Peter 1:2), persons who belong to God (1 Peter 2:9). We are loved by God (1 Thessalonians 1:4) and seated in heavenly realms (Ephesians 2:6). Our lives are now hidden with Christ in God (Colossians 3:3).

To date, the Roman Catholic Church has judged only one person born in the United States good enough to be called a saint: Mother Elizabeth Seton. The Roman Catholic Church applies that term only to individuals who have risen to some extraordinary degree of piety and goodness. But the New Testament calls every Christian a saint. In fact, as believers we have been raised by salvation into an extraordinary position, a high and holy place, as those who are peculiarly God's and who are set apart for His purposes.

God's *Purpose* for His Own

These opening verses of First Corinthians not only describe our position as Christians, but they state very clearly God's purpose for those of us who belong to Him. We believers are called to be holy.

Careful Bible scholars know that the words *to be* are not in the original Greek text. But they have been added quite properly by the translators, for that is the meaning intended by the original language. F.W. Grosheide says, "God . . . calls [the Corinthians] to walk according to their imputed holiness" (*Commentary on the First Epistle to the Corinthians,* page 24). Those of us who are set apart unto God through salvation are to be pure and clean and good in actual conduct and conversation.

A few years ago *Alliance Life* ran a story about a congregation that met for its services in what had once been a chicken coop. The congregation purchased the building, and from that moment on it was set apart to be a church building. It was dedicated for a holy use. Subsequently, however, the church members made sure the building no longer housed chickens. Instead, they repaired, remodeled, painted, furnished and then filled the building with people who worshiped the Lord there.

We Are to Be Filled with God's Praise

If we are Christians our lives are no longer to harbor lust, selfishness, bitterness, dishonesty, immorality and the like. Instead we are to be gracious, good, righteous. We are to be filled with the praises of God so that we honor and glorify Him.

This emphasis on practical holiness runs throughout the New Testament: "Do not let sin reign in your mortal body so that you obey its evil desires. . . . Rather . . . offer the parts of your body to [God] as instruments of righteousness" (Romans 6:12-13). "[God] condemned sin in sinful man, in order that the righteous requirements of the law might be fully met in us" (Romans 8:3-4). "We are God's workmanship, created in Christ Jesus to do good works, which God prepared in advance for us to do" (Ephesians 2:10).

Some people seem to think God saves us primarily so that we can go to heaven some day. Even some preaching seems to suggest that the fundamental purpose of salvation is personal happiness. In fact, God brought us to Himself through His Son primarily to make us holy.

God's *Provisions* for Us

We ought also to recognize from Paul's opening words to the Corinthians that God has given to us through salvation some magnificent provisions by which we can, in fact, live holy lives. Halfway through the greeting he comments: "In him you have been enriched in every way." Then he goes on to describe some of those riches. We should not miss the truth contained here because the provisions are crucial to the experience of practical, daily holiness.

Paul identifies four particular spiritual enrichments. The first is . . .

Spiritual Illumination

Paul says, "Our testimony about Christ was confirmed in you." Paul had gone to Corinth with divinely revealed truth. Through the illumination of the Holy Spirit, the Corinthians had comprehended God's Word. It was confirmed in them.

Paul later expands this thought. He says the person without the Spirit does not accept the things that come from the Spirit of God. They are foolishness to him or her. He or she cannot understand them (2:14). But Christians have the Spirit. We may understand what God has freely given to us (2:12).

I once became hopelessly lost while walking, as a tourist, through an old section of Athens, Greece. I had armed myself for my walking tour with a map I picked up at the hotel. But when I opened it up to try to determine where I was, I discovered it was all in Greek. I could not understand it. Fortunately, after a while a man came up to me and asked in

English if I was lost. Then he showed me on the map the way back to my hotel. If I had not received the assistance of someone who knew his way around the city, I might still be wandering those streets!

As we seek to make our way through all the issues and alternatives of life, we cannot by ourselves always know what we ought to do. This is especially true because we are constantly tempted by evil. We are confronted by satanic deceptions and we are lured by worldly influences that, if followed, would lead us astray.

But God has set His seal of ownership upon us by putting His Spirit in our hearts (2 Corinthians 1:22). That means the Holy Spirit is ever available to show us the right way, to give us divine direction, to enable us to understand God's will and to lead us in holy paths.

Spiritual illumination is the first great provision God makes available to us for practical, daily holiness.

Spiritual Strength

The second provision Paul mentions is spiritual strength. Paul says, "[God] will keep you strong to the end, so that you will be blameless on the day of our Lord Jesus Christ."

I can recall one particularly humiliating day when I was in junior high school. The instructor decided that all us boys in his gym class were going to climb ropes that hung from the ceiling of the gymnasium.

When my turn came I struggled even to get started upward. About one third of the way up my strength gave out and I could go no farther. I had to listen to that teacher's shouts of derision and endure the taunts of some of the boys in the class who had made it to the top. But I could go no farther.

Living holy lives may sometimes seem like that kind of an exercise. Indeed, none of us in our own strength can attain to genuine goodness, purity and godliness. But the Scriptures affirm that through the Holy Spirit's presence we have within us God's "incomparably great power" that He exerted "when he raised [Christ] from the dead and seated him at his right hand in the heavenly realms" (Ephesians 1:19-20).

Yes, God has put His own spiritual strength on call to help us live holy lives.

Spiritual Fellowship

Next Paul informs us that God has called us into fellowship with Christ. This, too, is crucial to our becoming holy, not just in our standing with God but in our practical daily living.

We become like those we spend time with. Husbands and wives become like each other in opinions, mannerisms, speech patterns, even in physical appearance. On occasion I have been in a room full of mature couples I did not know, people who were mingling socially in conversation. Before learning who belonged to whom, I have tried to match them just by their appearances. My guesses were more often right than wrong.

If we spend time with Jesus, we will begin to act like Him, think like Him, treat others as He treated people. We will take on His characteristics. And Christ was perfectly holy.

One of the greatest hindrances to personal holiness is busyness—the almost frantic pace of activity in which we find ourselves today. Busyness becomes a great obstacle to holiness because we have no time to sit at Jesus' feet, to focus upon His beauty, to listen to His voice, to open our souls to His presence.

Fellowship—deep, intimate communion with Christ—will transform our attitudes and alter our ways of behaving. Intimacy with Jesus thus is a third divine provision for holy living.

Spiritual Gifts

"Therefore you do not lack any spiritual gift," Paul tells the Corinthians in the opening paragraphs of his first letter to them (1:7). The subject of spiritual gifts is also crucial to holy living.

Holiness is not simply a matter of having a pure character, a clean heart and right conduct. A holy life also is a life of service to God, a life of doing good, a life of helping others. Paul assures the Corinthians that they will be gifted by the Holy Spirit for whatever ministry and service God calls them to.

Paul waits until later (1 Corinthians 12-14) to discuss spiritual gifts in greater detail. There we learn that the Holy Spirit imparts to each of us Christians some enabling, some ability that equips us for a ministry to the church as a whole, which is the body of Christ.

When I think of people I have known whom I readily would call holy, I most quickly think of kind individuals who had a powerful prayer ministry or those whose gracious speech and comforting care powerfully blessed some local church.

I think of teachers who knew and loved God's Word and who communicated it to others both in word and day-by-day living. But those traits and abilities marking such lives and making them memorable to me were the result of gifts given to them by the Holy Spirit. Spiritual gifts, then, are the fourth of the divine provisions to which the apostle refers in the opening verses of First Corinthians. Spiritual gifts are crucial to the kind of holy living God expects of us.

The Need to Be Filled

Initially, then, when we are saved and converted, we are set apart to God. We are positionally sanctified. And God who now owns us as His special possession wants us to be holy not just in position but in daily living and actual practice.

To bring that objective about, God the Father has provided for us spiritual illumination, spiritual power, spiritual fellowship and spiritual gifts. All four of these divine provisions are, of course, brought to us through the person and the presence of the Holy Spirit. That is why it is so utterly necessary for us to be filled with the Holy Spirit. The measure to which we are filled with the Spirit will determine how fully our lives are shaped by the spiritual illumination, spiritual power, spiritual fellowship and spiritual gifts that God has made available.

But no emphasis upon God's work in our lives at some point subsequent to conversion should blind us to our immediate sainthood. Even though the Corinthian Christians had a long way to go in terms of spiritual development, Paul told them they already were sanctified in Christ and enriched in every way.

The Word of God says this to us. And across the centuries these opening verses of First Corinthians speak to us this message: "Get out of the mud! Remember that you are saints."

God is our sanctification. The very nature of God passes into us. It is a divine holiness. Sanctification is not a degree of progress on the old plane. It puts us entirely upon a new plane! We pass out of the human into the divine. Henceforth it is not the best that we can be and do, but the best that God can be and do. It becomes natural for us to be holy, just as once it was natural for us to be sinful. We act according to the divine nature in us, and our choices, desires and ministries are spontaneous and free. Obedience is a luxury instead of a duty.

—A.B. Simpson—

CHAPTER	**Holiness**
10	**and**
	Sanctification

by Robert Willoughby

THE WEDDING WAS OVER. THE guests were assembling to enjoy the reception. My wife and I were seated with some of the bride's friends who, as it turned out, were total strangers both to the Christian faith and the legalistic tenets of the church in which the ceremony had just taken place.

As we were conversing, getting acquainted with each other, a man strode toward our table, a scowl on his face. Sensing what might be coming next, I braced myself.

"What gave you the biblical right to have rings placed on the fingers of the bride and groom?" he demanded of me in a loud voice. I could only guess the reaction of those with whom I was seated to the man's ill-timed and obtrusive question. I had already noticed the large, beautiful rings on their hands!

The brother (I'm sure he was a fellow-believer) was steeped in the notion that holiness is a code of rules governing external behavior (one of which I had brazenly broken) set down by his church. The scribes and Pharisees confronted Jesus with that kind of legalism, and He roundly condemned it.

Yet the concept continues to have many loyal and sincere disciples. Perhaps it is because obeying rules governing external behavior is easier than altering wrong attitudes or maintaining a loving disposition.

What other misconceptions of holiness are present among the Lord's people? I recall standing beside the bed of a sick Christian who had been greatly influenced by another definition of holiness. Looking up at me he asked in all solemnity, "Pastor, what is the difference between a sin and a fault?"

Knowing his background, I suspected immediately what he was getting at. He had been thinking on James' words to "confess your faults one to another . . . that ye may be healed" (James 5:16 KJV). Since he was *sanctified*, which for him meant that it was no longer possible to sin, he wanted to be sure that what he confessed was only a "fault" and not a "sin." But he was not quite sure of the difference!

I must admit to a certain perverted delight as I read the verse to him from my more contemporary translation, which uses *sins* instead of *faults* to translate the Greek word that Paul uses all the way through Romans for *sin!*

Holiness does not mean sinless perfection. The danger inherent in the teaching of sinless perfection is that people just "make mistakes." A man allegedly testified in one of F.B. Meyer's services that he had not sinned for 11 years. Meyer is reputed to have asked, "Is the brother's wife here?"

Nor does being sanctified mean "sitting on the lid" of our emotional pressure cooker or "gritting our teeth" to suppress the feelings we wish we didn't have. Nor is holiness what is acquired by secluding ourselves in a holy hideaway to prevent contamination from the evils of the outside world. It is not even the obtaining of some spectacular religious experience that produces a momentary sense of exultation, only to fade with the passing of time.

Biblical sanctification is none of the above.

What *Is* Sanctification?

What does it mean to be "sanctified"? How do we become "holy" persons? The word *holiness* describes both a position and a disposition. When we changed our mind about sin (repentance), believed on the Lord Jesus Christ (faith), and were given the new life of the Spirit (regeneration), we were united with Christ. God the Father, on the basis of Christ's atoning death, instantly credited to our account the perfect righteousness of Christ, blotting out our record of past sins, treating us as though we had never sinned (justification). By virtue of our new union with Christ, God declared us "saints" (holy ones), "set apart" (sanctified) unto Himself to be His human dwelling place through the Holy Spirit.

In the eyes of God, all that is true of Christ became true of us as believers in Christ. We can regard ourselves as having been crucified, buried, risen and exalted with Christ. The theologians call this "positional sanctification."

Not only does sanctification give us a new position in Christ, but through the Holy Spirit's patient process we receive a new *dis*position. The God who justified us through faith in His Son also called us to live holy lives. To all intents and purposes, He called us to be like Himself. "Be holy, because I am holy," God says (Leviticus 11:44). "Be imitators of God, . . . as dearly loved children" (Ephesians 5:1). Jesus said, "Love your enemies and pray for those who persecute you, that you may be sons of your Father in heaven" (Matthew 5:44-45). Saying "sons of your Father" is the Jewish way of saying "like your Father."

Often just by looking at a child we can tell who the child's parents are. Although the likeness is not perfect, we say, "He looks just like his father," or, "She looks just like her mother." Given the right circumstances, even the *dispositional* genes of the parent sometimes come embarrassingly to light in the behavior of the child!

So it is in the spiritual realm. Holiness means likeness to our Father in heaven or—what is the same thing—likeness to His Son, the Lord Jesus. This likeness will not be perfect until, at His coming again, Christ transforms "our lowly bodies so that they will be like his glorious body" (Philippians 3:21). But the process begins when we receive Christ into our life, and God has promised to complete the work He has started (Philippians 1:6). We call this transforming process *experiential sanctification*—the bringing about of practical, day-by-day holiness.

What Does Christ-likeness Look Like?

What does Christ-likeness look like? The answer to that question may be found in Paul's catalog of the "fruit of the Spirit" (Galatians 5:22-23). Really it is a description of Jesus' disposition.

As Christ-like persons we seek in *love* to minister

to the needs of others; we find Christ's *joy* deep within, triumphing over sorrow and sadness; we discover the *peace* of God—that quietness and confidence that give strength. We find in the midst of very trying circumstances Christ's *patience*; and when confronted by very difficult people, Christ's *longsuffering*. The lovely, God-like attribute of *kindness* blossoms forth while *goodness* (integrity), *faithfulness* (loyalty), *gentleness* and *self-control* grow in us.

With such a favored disposition a possibility, this yearning must well up in everyone of us:

> *I long, oh, I long to be holy,*
> *Conformed to [God's] will and His Word;*
> *I want to be gentle and Christ-like,*
> *I want to be just like my Lord.* (Simpson)

As believers we have confidence that we are justified freely by God's grace. We have seen a genuine dispositional change taking place within. But alas! we soon sense that there is lurking somewhere within us a kind of resistance to holiness. The changes that the Spirit of God has brought about are good and desirable, true. But we confess that the Christian life has not been one gloriously unbroken march upward. There have been failures! More than once we have had to call on that Advocate with the Father, Jesus Christ, the Righteous One, who is the propitiation for believers' sins as well as for the sins of the whole world. We begin to wonder,

What Is This Struggle within Me?

"Why this inner struggle," we want to know.

from Christlikeness? Has the Holy Spirit departed from me? Are there times when He arbitrarily deserts His dwelling place?"

What is the cause of this downward pull that every honest Christian feels to some degree? To understand it, we need to recall a word found in the Scriptures. It is the word *flesh,* sometimes translated "sinful nature." In Greek, it is *sarx.* The Bible says that all of us at one time found ourselves "gratifying the cravings of our sinful nature [flesh, *sarx*] and following its desires and thoughts" (Ephesians 2:3-4). Before the Spirit of Christ entered us, the general inclination of our lives was to gratify the *sarx,* the flesh.

What is this power called the flesh? That kindly British preacher, J. Sidlow Baxter, in his little book, *A New Call to Holiness,* describes the flesh as "not some separable, eradicable, evil entity within us, but rather the animal and selfish inclination, predisposition, propensity inhering in and coextensive with our moral nature." He could have shortened it to say the flesh is our fallen animal instincts and appetites. Before we were born again of the Spirit, *sarx* sat as king of our lives. Yielding to *sarx* was habitual.

Just prior to spelling out the fruit of the Spirit, the Bible offers us a graphic picture of the flesh. To some extent, one or more of these manifestations of our animal instincts and appetites characterized our pre-Christian life: "sexual immorality [fornication, adultery], impurity [unclean fantasies] and debauchery [pornography]; idolatry [with 'I' as the god] and witchcraft [the occult and drug scene]; hatred,. discord [a life ruled by bitterness, malice and strife], jealousy [coveting another's talents], fits

109

and strife], jealousy [coveting another's talents], fits of rage [the control of others by a violent temper], selfish ambition {finding self-worth in trampling over others to get to the top}, dissensions, factions [insisting on having our own way, regardless of the consequences] and envy [begrudging how God has blessed others]; drunkenness, orgies and the like." It is not a pretty picture!

With the entrance of the Holy Spirit into our life, the flesh is by no means annihilated. We are now "in Christ . . . a new creation" (2 Corinthians 5:17), true. But from time to time we still feel what the Puritan writers called "the motions of the flesh." We have two forces within us, both vying for control: the flesh, which prior to salvation dominated our life, and the Spirit, who desires to be in total control. The struggle we sense is the war between flesh and Spirit. So we need to ask:

What Does a Holy Person Do with the Flesh?

God is very clear on what we as believers should do with our flesh. *Put it to death!* The Scriptures say exactly that: "Put to death, therefore, whatever belongs to your earthly nature" (Colossians 3:5). "If by the Spirit you put to death the misdeeds of the body, you will live" (Romans 8:13).

Notice how these Scriptures call for a decision of the will. If we would be sanctified "through and through" (1 Thessalonians 5:23), there must come a moment of spiritual crisis in which we recognize our own helplessness to overcome the flesh. Repenting for our past sins, we choose to solemnly present ourselves to God, surrendering body, mind and spirit to Him, inviting the Holy Spirit to take full control.

That surrender must be renewed day by day in a continual yielding of ourselves to the Lordship of Christ, counting ourselves dead to sin and alive to God in Christ Jesus. As we choose to "keep in step with the Spirit" (Galatians 5:25), God will enable us to say No to the deeds of the flesh and Yes to the disposition of Christ. He will enable us to "put off {our} old self, which is being corrupted by its deceitful desires" and to "put on the new self, created to be like God in true righteousness and holiness" (Ephesians 4:22-23).

How Can I Be Like Christ?

That leaves us with the big question: *How can I be like Christ?* We have said that a holy, sanctified life is neither a sinlessly perfect one nor a sternly legalistic one. The sinful nature is to be neither resolutely suppressed nor cloistered from all possibility of temptation. A sanctified life is one in which the risen Christ, through the indwelling of His Holy Spirit, is transforming disposition and behavior into His own.

I confess unabashedly that I like to watch professional baseball. It is by far my favorite spectator sport! I enjoy its intricacy—the signals, the attempts of one manager to outwit the other, the planning ahead. I relish the 90-mile-per-hour fast balls, the shortstop's leaping stabs, the superb double plays, the long throws home, the sliders, the curves, the home runs. And the pros make it all look so easy!

My favorite pitcher is Juan Guzman of Toronto.

Sometimes I imagine myself on the pitcher's mound. But then I quickly realize there is no way that I could pitch like Guzman—unless—unless, by some strange alchemy, Guzman the pro could get his body inside mine so that his powerful muscles merged with my weaker ones, his strong pitching arm blended with my unpracticed one, his sharp eye fused with my less-trained one.

As I walk out to the mound, the Guzman inside me whispers, "Look, just surrender your body to me and let me do what you can't. I'll do the pitching."

The cheering crowd sees me—Willoughby—pitching a remarkable game of baseball. But Guzman and I both know it is not I who am playing the game but the pro whose being has taken over mine.

Imagine what would happen if after a few great games I would say to my pro, "Look, Guzman, I think I can go it alone today. You just stay here in the dugout and *I* will pitch today. I know how it's done, and I'm sure I can do it."

And Guzman lets me go out there and face the batters alone while he thinks to himself, *I'll just have to let that chap learn the hard way that apart from me he can't do it.* And of course I fail miserably, and the Dome laughs me to scorn and wonders what in the world happened.

When it comes to holiness, it's only something like that. But it is undeniably true that living a Christ-like life is only possible as I completely yield myself totally to the Holy Spirit, who inhabits my frail house. When I become self-reliant and think that by my own cleverness or will power or ability to imitate I can be like Jesus, the Spirit steps aside for the moment and lets me discover anew that without Him I can do nothing. I have to know that it is not I, but Christ who lives in me.

That is the secret of a holy life. Sanctification is nothing other than the risen Lord Jesus Christ living His life in me by the Holy Spirit. As I continually yield myself totally to Him, He is in process of transforming me into His likeness.

I must nourish the life of the Spirit day by day by steeping my mind and heart in the Scriptures, by engaging in Spirit-imparted prayer, in regular worship with God's people, in putting myself under the faithful ministry of a Bible-teaching pastor, by serving Christ and His church with the gifts the Spirit gives me, and by sharing my faith with unbelievers as I am confronted with Spirit-arranged opportunities.

What a marvelously full salvation God has provided for all of us who believe on His Son! He offers a free pardon from sin, total acceptance in Christ, a new spiritual position, separation from the world unto Himself, and the ability to live a holy life through the indwelling of the Holy One Himself.

I remember the day when in the attic of our home I made that full surrender of myself to Christ and opened my whole being, by faith, to the Holy Spirit. A whole new life of praise, a whole new life of victory over the flesh opened up before me. I felt that I could never sin again!

But that was not true. I did sin. I needed to know . . .

What to Do about Failure

What if, as Spirit-filled people, we sin? We need

to remember two important truths. First, although we may have lost temporarily the conscious awareness of fellowship with God, our position in Christ has not changed. We need not despair that all is lost.

The One who "always lives to intercede" for us (Hebrews 7:25) stands as our advocate before the Father. As Charles Wesley so fittingly put it, "Before the throne my Surety stands: / My name is written on His hands." Satan would do his best to condemn us, as would our own conscience. But we need to remember this Scripture: "Who will bring any charge against those whom God has chosen? It is God who justifies. Who is he that condemns? Christ Jesus, who died—more than that, who was raised to life—is at the right hand of God and is also interceding for us" (Romans 8:33-34).

Second, the Holy Spirit invites us to come immediately to God's throne of grace and find pardon. His Word reminds us that "If we confess our sins, he is faithful and just and will forgive us our sins and purify us from all unrighteousness" (1 John 1:9). Our adversary Satan would have us delay our coming for pardon until we have done appropriate penance. "Surely," he hisses mockingly, "you must atone for your own sin. How can you be sure that God will forgive you?"

Again the Holy Spirit brings to our remembrance these assuring words: "Praise the Lord, O my soul, . . . / who forgives all your sins" (Psalm 103:2-3).

In view of our Heavenly Father's rich provision for life and godliness, the hymn prayer attributed to Mary D. James seems most appropriate:

My spirit, soul and body, Jesus I give to Thee,

A consecrated offering Thine evermore to be.
My all is on the altar; Lord, I am all Thine own;
Oh, may my faith ne'er falter! Lord, keep
  me Thine alone.

Oh, blissful self-surrender to live, my Lord,
  by Thee!
Now, Son of God, my Savior, live out Thy life
  in me.
I'm Thine, O blessed Jesus, washed in Thy
  precious blood,
Sealed by Thy Holy Spirit, a sacrifice to God.

**God commands us to be holy. He calls
us to be holy. He will not excuse anyone
from holiness. We have no right to call
ourselves His children if we continue to
live in sin. "Shall we go on sinning so that
grace may increase? By no means!"
(Romans 6:1-2). By no means are you to
continue in sin. There are not two classes
of Christians between which you may
choose. There are no options here. Every
child of God is called to be holy.**
—A.B. Simpson—

Holiness and Divine Healing

by K. Neill Foster

HOLINESS AND DIVINE HEALING? ARE they related? The answers are both yes and sometimes no. A church congregation determined to give over an entire day to pray for one of its members, a woman greatly loved by all, who had been afflicted by an illness that contorted her body. In that condition, she was brought into the assembly of believers on a bed.

The congregation was aware of the biblical instruction: "Confess your sins to each other and pray one for each other so that you may be healed" (James 5:16). Confession, then prayer. So before addressing the physical need of their afflicted member, the people in obedience to the Word of God first began confessing their sins to one another.

What transpired that day was amazing. As the members of the congregation advanced in practical holiness by confessing their sins to each other, the twisted body of their beloved fellow-believer gradually straightened. By the end of the day she was healed. It had been a gradual but visible healing directly related to purity among the believers. In that church that day, physical healing was clearly connected with holiness, even as it is in James 5:16.

Some General Propositions

Before we go farther, we need to set out some general propositions in reference to healing.

The first: *God heals.* Healing is a reflection of God's nature and character. He told the Israelites, "I am the LORD, who heals you" (Exodus 15:26).

The second: *Satan heals.* The Scriptures inform us that the coming "lawless one will be in accordance with the work of Satan displayed in all kinds of counterfeit miracles, signs and wonders" (2 Thessalonians 2:9).

The third proposition: *Healing sometimes comes to non-Christians as a beneficence of God.* Naaman, the Assyrian general afflicted with leprosy, had no redemptive or covenantal right to be healed. Devoid of any kind of holiness, he was nonetheless healed. "He went down and dipped himself in the Jordan seven times, as the man of God had told him, and his flesh was restored and became clean like that of a young boy" (2 Kings 5:14).

The fourth: *Healing for Christians is the children's bread* (see Mark 7:27). The sick person is to "call the elders of the church to pray over him and anoint him with oil in the name of the Lord. And the prayer offered in faith will make the sick person well; the Lord will raise him up. If he has sinned, he will be forgiven" (James 5:14-15). When confession of sin is followed by the prayer of faith, the Lord will heal the sick person.

Let me deal with each of these propositions in a little greater depth.

God Heals

The catalog of healing in both the Old and New Testaments is extensive. The first recorded instance of healing is of Abimelech's household. Abimelech, a highly-principled Negev chieftain, had innocently taken Sarah, who Abraham said was his sister, into his harem. God set the record straight by speaking to Abimelech in a dream, and Abimelech at once restored Sarah, with whom he had had no relations, to Abraham. The Bible says, "Then Abraham prayed to God, and God healed Abimelech, his wife and his slave girls so they could have children again, for the Lord had closed up every womb in Abimelech's household because of Abraham's wife Sarah" (Genesis 20:17-18).

The four New Testament Gospels detail the healing ministry of Jesus Christ. He who was the perfect expression of divine compassion (see Mark 6:34) "healed the sick" (Matthew 8:16). "Jesus went throughout Galilee, teaching in their synagogues, preaching the good news of the kingdom, and healing every disease and sickness among the people" (Matthew 4:23).

If indeed Jesus today is the unchanged Jesus of the Gospels and the New Testament (see Hebrews 13:8), dare we cast any doubt at all upon His ability or His willingness to heal? Surely not.

At the same time, we must confess also that God is sovereign. Not all who wish to be healed are healed. Apparently only one man among the "great number" of sufferers at Jerusalem's Bethesda pool found relief (John 5:1-9). Ever since Adam, death is the appointed lot of humankind (Psalm 90:10;

Hebrews 9:27), and death implies physical maladies of one sort or another that God in His sovereignty declines to touch.

Satan Heals

Incidences of Satan's power to heal can be found both in the Scriptures and in contemporary occult and cultic religions. Pharaoh's magicians had ability—for a time—to compete with the power of God exhibited by Moses and Aaron (Exodus 7:11, 22; 8:7). We have already noted that in a future time Satan will display "all kinds of counterfeit miracles" through the "lawless one" who is to come. In Revelation, the "beast coming out of the sea," a part of Satan's evil triumvirate, "seemed to have had a fatal wound" on one of its heads, "but the fatal wound had been healed" (Revelation 13:1-3).

Kurt Koch, the late German theologian, spent a lifetime of research gathering case studies affirming the reality—and the debilitating aftereffects—of occult healing. Witch doctors, shamans and *curanderos* in all parts of the world attest to the presence of supernatural healing not derived from Almighty God.

The noted Bible commentator, Matthew Henry, suggests how physical healing, normally a benefit, might come from Satan, the prince of darkness. Commenting on Luke 11:17-26, Henry notes that Satan is not above military feints and strategic withdrawals (healings) if his overall cause can be thereby advanced. His nature remains the same. He is a murderer and a liar, intent on humankind's eternal destruction.

That such counter-kingdom healings are disconnected from holiness should be self-evident. The powers of darkness are the antithesis of holiness. But malevolent spirits on occasion usurp for themselves the right to heal.

Healing, a Benevolent Gift of God

Naaman, the leprous Assyrian general, was not of the house of Israel. As a stranger to God's covenant with Abraham and the patriarchs, he had no right to expect healing. As far as we know, he possessed no imparted holiness because of any faith in God. Yet he demonstrated a certain audacity born out of desperation. He went to see the prophet Elisha. Although dipping seven times in the Jordan River was not Naaman's idea of a cleansing experience, he did so and was healed of his incurable disease.

In the New Testament there is the Canaanite woman, a Gentile, who argued before Jesus that just as the dogs under the table have rights to the crumbs, so she had a right to claim healing for her daughter, and so she did (Matthew 15:22-28).

In recent years there have been large evangelistic crusades in third world countries. Often prayer for the sick is an integral part of the crusades. Credible witnesses repeatedly attest that remarkable healings take place in the name of Jesus Christ. Curiously, local Christians often complain that they are not healed.

Why does God choose to heal pagans and those who follow false religions? The only reasonable answer is that healings among unbelievers are intended to display the power of Jesus Christ and bring people to repentance—and they often do just that. They are "Naaman-healings," "Canaanite-healings" among people who have no covenantal or redemptive relationship with the Savior.

Healing Is the Children's Bread

Believers in Jesus Christ are members of His church, His invisible, universal Body. As such, they are under godly discipline. They are within a holy order. They are under a biblical mandate to pursue holiness, without which no one will see the Lord (Hebrews 12:14).

Thank God, a route to healing exists for them, too. But it lies within the body of the church. In *The Gospel of Healing* A.B. Simpson makes the point that Christians must be dealt with spiritually before physical healing can become a reality. "God works from within outward," he writes. "There is a close relation between the state of the soul and the body."

In saying that healing is the right of every child of God, we need to keep three points in mind.

First, *healing rests in the redemptive work of Jesus Christ*. "By his wounds we are healed" (Isaiah 53:5). Lest the reference to Jesus Christ is in doubt, the New Testament confirms it:

> When evening came, many who were demon-possessed were brought to [Jesus], and he drove out the spirits with a word and healed all the sick. This was to fulfill what was spoken through the prophet Isaiah:
>
> "He took up our infirmities
> and carried our diseases."
> (Matthew 8:16-17)

Second, *healing reaches the sick and afflicted through the indwelling Person of Jesus Christ.* One of the mysteries of the Christian faith is that Jesus Christ indwells believers. Paul expresses it, "Christ in you, the hope of glory" (Colossians 1:27).

As Jesus Christ indwells believers and works through them, He often expresses His healing intent, His healing compassion. Indeed, His healing touch is extended through them to suffering humanity on every side.

Third, *healing is appropriated through acts of holiness within the church body.* "Confess your sins one to another," James said. Could anything be clearer? Confession is to "say the same thing." In colloquial parlance, it is to tell it like it is. When Christians start doing that before one another, healings begin to take place. The personal pursuit of holiness creates fertile ground out of which the prayer of faith may quickly spring.

As an elder in my local church, I am aware that many times the sick are not healed when we pray. Were we to determine to fulfill the conditions laid down in James 5:14-16 as exactly as we know, I am convinced that many, many more of the sick among us would receive healing in Christ's name.

Conclusion

Two instances of healing have etched themselves on my mind and heart. The first took place in 1963. A slender, teenaged girl had strayed away from God and become a habitation of foul spirits. The girl's violence as we prayed with her was at times such that it took five strong men to control her.

We commanded the demons to leave, and some did. But the remaining powers refused to budge. The Christian workers who had gathered to help were stymied. Our prayers and commands seemed of no avail.

But then quietly and without ostentation, the Christian workers began to confess their sins. Not big sins. They were "the little foxes / that ruin the vineyards" (Song of Songs 2:15) in the lives of dedicated servants of Christ. But they were sins nonetheless.

I cannot forget what happened next. The demons who had refused to obey our commands and before whom our prayers seemed unavailing began of their own accord to convulse the girl and then leave, one after another. As we confessed our sins, as we sought holiness of life, the girl who was so grievously bound was delivered.

The second instance reinforces my point about holiness and healing. At a summer camp meeting my wife and I were counseling with a woman. She was bound by a "Jesus" who was not the Lord Jesus Christ. This "other Jesus" (see 2 Corinthians 11:4) was a sexy, sensual Jesus who defied both the woman's prayers and our efforts to dislodge it. Finally, in desperation, I began to pray inwardly. I began to confess my sin.

That sin, by the way, was the love of money. My role at the conference was to raise the expense budget. When this woman's husband had announced his intention to be absent on "check night," the special night when we raised most of the budget, I was inwardly, sinfully critical. I wanted his participation on check night.

My love of money was a serious offense to a holy

God. It was serious enough to hinder the deliverance of the man's wife, whom Satan had bound. But as I confessed my sin silently and quietly, the sensual Jesus-spirit suddenly departed. The effect was so dramatic that both my wife and the other woman turned to me.

"What did you do?" they asked almost in unison. My embarrassment was total. But I finally told them what I have just written.

"If I had cherished sin in my heart, / the Lord would not have listened" (Psalm 66:18).

"He who conceals his sins does not prosper, / but whoever confesses and renounces them finds mercy" (Proverbs 28:13).

"Confess your sins to each other and pray for each other so that you may be healed" (James 5:16).

Burn on, O fire of God, burn on,
Till all my dross is burned away.
Burn up the dregs of self and sin;
Prepare me for the testing day.
—A.B. Simpson—

CHAPTER	# Holiness and the Lord's Return
12	

by Wendell K. Grout

I S THE DOCTRINE OF THE Second Advent really just strange speculation by religious people looking for "pie in the sky by and by"? Is it an escape mechanism detached from reality, invented by people who shrink from the vicissitudes of life? It is without moral substance?

In fact, the teaching of our Lord's return to earth has vast spiritual and moral overtones. Someone has noted that every New Testament mention of Jesus' second coming has in it practical application to the believer. It is far more than an interesting future event providing curious minds with some fascinating mysteries to explore.

One of the great moral qualities vitally connected with our Savior's return is holiness. Indeed, the greatest manifestations of Jesus' holiness await His return. Whatever of holiness we have seen or experienced to this point is a mere shadow of what is to come.

In view of Christ's return to earth, I am suggesting that holiness has a *personal meaning,* a *millennial meaning* and an *eternal meaning.*

Holiness Has a Personal Meaning

In relation to the return of the Lord Jesus Christ, I experience holiness in two ways. I experience progressive holiness in my personal anticipation of His return. I also will experience perfect holiness in my personal glorification at His return.

Let's consider that first thought. Well-known Scriptures support the idea that my anticipation of the coming of Christ has a stimulating effect on my spiritual life.

For example, note this verse: "Make every effort to live in peace with all men and to be holy; without holiness no one will see the Lord" (Hebrews 12:14). Holiness as a character quality and a life style is essential if I am to see the Lord—mystically now and actually later. Holiness is not an experience reserved for a few extraordinary saints. It is for all who genuinely believe in Christ and desire to please Him.

Here is another Scripture: "When [Jesus Christ] appears, we shall be like him, for we shall see him as he is. Everyone who has this hope in him purifies himself, just as he is pure" (1 John 3:2-3). If I have the hope of seeing the Lord Jesus face to face, I will purify myself even as He is pure. I will develop an intense intolerance for sin. I will desire to reflect the pure and holy character of the Lord whose name I bear. Regrettably, many professing Christians seem more bent on having the Lord make them happy than holy.

Intense Focus

No Scripture focuses as intensely on holiness in

the light of Jesus' return as First Peter 1:13-16:

> Prepare your minds for action; be self-controlled; set your hope fully on the grace to be given you when Jesus Christ is revealed. As obedient children, do not conform to the evil desires you had when you lived in ignorance. But just as he who called you is holy, so be holy in all you do; for it is written: "Be holy, because I am holy."

Holy conduct that reflects God's holy character is the mandate for all believers. This holiness doesn't come without some very earnest and disciplined effort. We are to be mentally alert. We are to be self-controlled. We are to rest our hope on the grace that will be ours when Christ is revealed. We are to obey God. We are to reject evil desires. Above all, we are to respond to His example of holiness by being holy in all our conduct.

We will never be more holy than we desire to be. Nor are there any shortcuts, any simple little formulas. Holiness must be an ongoing, diligent pursuit.

Other Powerful Words

God inspired Peter with other powerful words on this truth of holiness and the return of Christ:

> The day of the Lord will come like a thief. The heavens will disappear with a roar; the elements will be destroyed by fire, and the earth and everything in it will be laid bare.
>
> Since everything will be destroyed in this way, what kind of people ought you to be? You ought to

live holy and godly lives as you look forward to the day of God and speed its coming. That day will bring about the destruction of the heavens by fire, and the elements will melt with the heat. But in keeping with his promise, we are looking forward to a new heaven and a new earth, the home of righteousness.

So then, dear friends, since you are looking forward to this, make every effort to be found spotless, blameless and at peace with him. (2 Peter 3:10-14)

The return of Jesus will introduce the awful Day of the Lord that Peter here so graphically describes. In light of what is to happen, Peter urges God's people to "live holy and godly lives." Because the material world as we know it will pass away, he admonishes them to care for what is permanent—their eternal souls.

Note also that they are to look for "a new heaven and a new earth, the home of righteousness." And how are they to prepare for this new creation? By making "every effort to be found spotless, blameless and at peace with him." We must develop the character *now* that will suit that holy place *then.* More about this later.

I cite one final Scripture that links holiness and the Lord's return to our personal lives. It is a prayer Paul prays for the Christians in Thessalonica: "May the Lord make your love increase and overflow for each other and for everyone else, just as ours does for you. May he strengthen your hearts so that you will be blameless and holy in the presence of our God and Father when our Lord Jesus comes with all his holy ones" (1 Thessalonians 3:12-13).

Again, we see the vital relationship between our holiness and the coming of Jesus Christ. Only the Lord can "establish [our] hearts blameless in holiness" (NKJV).

Perfect Holiness at Christ's Return

We have considered progressive holiness in anticipation of the Lord's return. Now let's think about the perfect holiness that we will experience in our glorification at His return.

The Bible clearly speaks about this in Ephesians 5:25-27. Note first that "Christ loved the church and gave himself up for her." Second, He made her "holy, cleansing her by the washing with water through the word." Third, He will "present her to himself as a radiant church, without stain or wrinkle or any other blemish." The final words of description for Christ's "bride," the church, are that she will be "holy and blameless."

The text certainly underlines the fact that our holiness finds its source in the Lord Jesus Himself. It began when He gave His life for us on the cross; it continues with the cleansing effect of His Word; it will be climaxed when we in glorious perfection become His holy bride at Jesus' return.

John, the prophet of Patmos, adds his exciting description of this wonderful future event:

> Let us rejoice and be glad
>   and give him glory!
> For the wedding of the Lamb has come,
>   and his bride has made herself ready.
> Fine linen, bright and clean,
>   was given her to wear. (Revelation 19:7-8)

The Bible declares: "Our citizenship is in heaven. And we eagerly await a Savior from there, the Lord Jesus Christ, who, by the power that enables him to bring everything under his control, will transform our lowly bodies so that they will be like his glorious body" (Philippians 3:20-21).

When Jesus returns, we will receive new bodies. They will be bodies fitted for glory just like the resurrected body of our Lord. Our bodies are a vital part of God's redemption (Romans 8:23). God redeems every part of us.

At the same time our bodies are glorified, our souls—the inner us—will be perfected: "When [Jesus Christ] appears, we shall be like him, for we shall see him as he is" (1 John 3:2). At the present, we are looking at Christ by faith and in the Word of God. Progressively we are being transformed by the Spirit into His image.

The more we look *at* Jesus, the more we look *like* Jesus (2 Corinthians 3:18). This will continue until He returns. Then we will see our glorious Lord "face to face" (1 Corinthians 13:12). Immediately we shall be changed into His image. At last we will be perfectly holy, delivered from the power of sin forever.

Now it is the progression of holiness. When Jesus comes for us, it will be the perfection of holiness.

Holiness Has a Millennial Meaning

When Christ the King returns, it will be to establish His kingdom. In view of this coming kingdom and our Lord's righteous rule, holiness has a millennial meaning.

According to Revelation 20, our Lord will reign a

thousand years over all the nations of the earth. In *The Moody Handbook of Theology*, Dr. Paul P. Enns describes the period of Christ's millennial kingdom:

> The conditions during the Millennium will depict a perfect environment physically and spiritually. It will be a time of peace (Micah 4:2-4; Isaiah 32:17-18); joy (Isaiah 61:7, 10); comfort (Isaiah 40:1-2); and no poverty (Amos 9:13-15) or sickness (Isaiah 35:5-6). Because only the believers will enter the Millennium, it will be a time of righteousness (Matthew 25:37; Psalm 24:3-4); obedience (Jeremiah 31:33); holiness (Isaiah 35:8); truth (Isaiah 65:16) and fullness of the Holy Spirit (Joel 2:28-29). (Page 393)

Quite obviously this will be the most unusual period in all the history of the world. The Lord Jesus will accomplish by His coming what humankind has failed to accomplish in thousands of years. Indeed, the reign of Christ will begin in the ashes of Armageddon, the last and bloodiest war of all time—a war against the Son of God Himself.

The Kingdom Will Be Holy

One of the qualities of this perfect kingdom will be holiness. If one word could describe humankind's social, religious and political behavior throughout history it would be the term *unholy*. But consider the following:

- Christ will rule from the *holy* hill of Zion (Psalm 2:6)
- He will have the presence of the *Holy* Spirit

131

upon Him (Isaiah 11:1-2)

• People will offer exuberant praise to the *Holy* One of Israel in their midst (Isaiah 12:6)

• Gentiles will worship in the *holy* mount at Jerusalem (Isaiah 27:13; 56:6-7)

• There will be a *holy* sanctuary in the *holy* city, Jerusalem (Joel 3:17; Ezekiel 45:1-4)

• The *Holy* Spirit will be poured out upon the people (Isaiah 32:15; Joel 2:28)

• In the renewed and blossoming earth there will be a highway of *holiness,* and nothing unclean will traverse it (Isaiah 35:8)

• The *Holy* One of Israel will save His people out of the nations (Isaiah 43:1-7)

• The people of the kingdom will be called the *holy* people, the redeemed of the Lord (Isaiah 62:12)

• There will be no hurt and no destruction in the Lord's *holy* mountain (Isaiah 65:25)

Added to that list are some curious words in Zechariah 14:20-21. "On that day HOLY TO THE LORD will be inscribed on the bells of the horses, and the cooking pots in the LORD'S house will be like the sacred bowls in front of the altar. Every pot in Jerusalem and Judah will be holy to the LORD Almighty." It would seem that under the holy scepter of the Lord Jesus, everything—even common and ordinary things—will be set apart to God's use and serve a holy purpose.

Someone has said, "The Lord delights in using common people and common things in uncommon ways." If the Lord can use bells and pots as a means of expressing His holiness, how much more can He use my life!

Holiness Has an Eternal Meaning

The millennial reign of Christ introduces us to the eternal reign of Christ. The millennium sets the stage for and ushers in the Kingdom of God that will continue, world without end. It bridges Jesus' reign in time and His reign in eternity, from the earthly Jerusalem to the New Jerusalem, from limited earthbound dimensions to unlimited, eternal dimensions. Here is John's description of the new heaven and the new earth:

> I saw a new heaven and a new earth, for the first heaven and the first earth had passed away, and there was no longer any sea. I saw the Holy City, the new Jerusalem, coming down out of heaven from God. . . . And I heard a loud voice from the throne saying, "Now the dwelling of God is with men, and he will live with them. They will be his people, and God himself will be with them and be their God. He will wipe every tear from their eyes. There will be no more death or mourning or crying or pain, for the old order of things has passed away."
>
> He who was seated on the throne said, "I am making everything new!" (Revelation 21:1-5)

The Scriptures leave us in no doubt concerning the holy character of the New Jerusalem. Twice it is called the *Holy* City (21:2, 10). It is a city with walls (21:12). Walls speak of strong protection from any enemies that might disturb the holy condition and perfect environment of the city.

But the 12 gates will be open (21:12,25)! Guar-

133

dian angels keep the city perfectly secure, but those within will have no "fortress feeling." Each of us will have open and ready access to our glorious Lord and all the rich provision He has made for us. We will enjoy perfect security and perfect liberty!

The city will have strong and beautiful foundations (Revelation 21:14). They speak of the city's enduring quality. Its holy character is fixed, unchanging, not subject to deterioration.

The entire New Jerusalem will be the temple of God (21:22). We will not go some place to worship. We will worship everywhere and at all times because we will never be removed from God's templeing Presence! God's glory will fill the city with eternal radiance (21:23; 22:5).

Finally, "the throne of God and of the Lamb will be in the city" (22:3). The eternal city will be ruled as a theocracy forever! Under this beneficent and holy rule, we will serve God with gladness forever.

Summary

Holiness and the Lord's return. The climax of our spiritual journey as believers is ahead! The best is future! Our delight in that day of the Lord's return is tied to our progress in holiness here and now. Holy will describe Jesus' millennial rule. Holy characterizes the New Jerusalem. Holy is to characterize us as we anticipate Jesus' glorious appearing.

Three times in the concluding chapter of the Bible, our Lord says He is coming quickly. What an encouraging promise! What hope it gives us! What a glorious prospect for those of us who long for holiness in its fullest expression!

Even so, come, Lord Jesus!

CHAPTER 13

Christo-centric Holiness

by Donald A. Wiggins

AFTER DARING GERMAN CONSPIRATORS IN July, 1944, almost succeeded in assassinating Adolf Hitler, the fiendish dictator installed tight security measures among his closest advisers. The narrow escape had pushed him to the point of paranoia.

Reeling from the Japanese surprise attack on Pearl Harbor, the United States government, fearing acts of subversion, confined thousands of Japanese-Americans in detention camps until the war ended. It was an extreme action later admitted to have been illegal.

Over the centuries Christians have battled three powerful enemies bent on their spiritual downfall. These they identify as the world, the flesh and the devil. The world and the devil are formidable enough, overcome only in the power of the One who conquered them both. The third—the flesh—operates much like a subversive, sabotaging from the inside. As the statement made famous in World War II says, "We have met the enemy, and he is us!"

The New Testament first named this internal foe. In Romans 8:1-11 Paul explains that "the flesh" (not "sinful nature," as in the New International Version) is that sphere of life characterized by sinful opposition to God. Those who set their minds on the flesh and live according to its corrupt desires cannot please God (8:5, 8). For them the "life and peace" of the Spirit-controlled mind is foreign (8:6).

In reality, all human beings not controlled by the Holy Spirit are dominated by the flesh. Sinful cravings and desires within them control their actions (see Ephesians 2:1-3). Their flesh orients them as a gyroscope toward a horrible list of sinful acts (see Galatians 5:19-21). Paul describes this condition as spiritual death (Ephesians 2:1). It subjects them to God's wrath (2:3).

It Need Not Be the Final Chapter

But this condition need not be the final chapter of any person's story. Those who trust in the Lord Jesus Christ to save them, God graciously raises out of spiritual death into new spiritual life (2:4-6). With their sins forgiven, they move out from under God's wrath into His favor. Old things pass away and everything becomes new under the ownership of the Lord Jesus Christ (2 Corinthians 5:17).

One of the most striking effects of spiritual rebirth is that the new believers are united with Christ. Once they were far away, now they are joined to Him.

Jesus' disciples were the first to hear this truth. Jesus said that though He had been with them, after His resurrection He would be *in* them by the Holy Spirit. "You will realize that I am in my Father, and you are in me, and I am in you," He told them (John 14:20).

This theme runs through the subsequent preaching and teaching of the apostles. Christ indwells His people, the church, in the person of the Holy Spirit (1 Corinthians 3:16-17). Christians reside "in Christ" so that they may be conformed to His image (Romans 8:29) and reflect His glory to the world (2 Corinthians 3:18).

Paul states it succinctly but clearly in First Corinthians 1:30:

> It is because of him [the Father who called you to salvation] that you are in Christ Jesus, who has become for us wisdom from God—that is, our righteousness, holiness and redemption.

It is unfortunate that not all Christians understand the significance of this truth. I find few who understand that they are joined with Christ who is their holiness. I find few who grasp the fact that He inhabits them and they live in him.

Two Extremes

This tragic lapse evidences itself in several ways, but particularly two. It leads some to wrongly assume that sheer exertion of their wills through strict discipline will yield a holy life. But then they discover that even their finest efforts fall short. They conclude in frustration that they never will be holy because they cannot summon enough willpower.

Others go to the opposite extreme. They seem to believe that a gracious God overlooks habitual sin.

After all, no one is perfect. By their actions they indicate that God and the church will just have to tolerate their continued sinful behavior.

Such a distortion of grace underestimates the power of Christ to change them! To them, as to their first-century counterparts who suggested, "Let sin increase so that grace may increase," Paul counters, "May it never be!" (Romans 6:2, NASB).

Neither making excuses for sin nor exerting superhuman effort to improve is the solution. The real answer for believers who aspire to holy living is the recognition that Jesus Christ is their sanctification!

A First-Person Testimony

The most convincing invitation into this truth is the testimony of one who has personally experienced it. Listen to what Paul says:

> *I have been crucified with Christ and I no longer live, but Christ lives in me. The life I live in the body, I live by faith in the Son of God, who loved me and gave himself for me.* (Galatians 2:20)

Could Paul have been exaggerating for the purpose of asserting a super-spiritual authority over his wavering Galatian disciples? Or was this really his experience and can such a union with Christ be a reality for every believer?

The context shows that Paul's words cannot be dismissed as hyperbole. The law was perfect, true. But it was powerless to justify him before God. Paul failed, as have all others who try to gain righteousness by keeping the law. Though he was willing to obey the law, his flesh was a counterweight he could not overcome. For Paul, the *only* way to overcome the flesh was to participate in the life of Christ with whom he was united.

All of us who would be holy must arrive at this same point of realization. The internal enemy that dominates and corrupts cannot be overcome by sheer effort. We will see that God has appointed Jesus Christ to replace the dominion of the flesh with His own presence and power. As it was for Paul, so today. All true personal experiences of sanctification have Christ at their center.

From Paul's testimony in Galatians 2:20 we may draw out three great principles that constitute the way we break free from slavery to the flesh. Each presupposes our new life in Christ Jesus. Each presupposes our union with Christ Jesus. Taken together they speak powerfully to a church preoccupied with many good things, but desperately in need of revival.

I have named these principles a life of *identification* with Christ, a life of *possession* by Christ and a life of *appropriation* of Christ.

Identification with Christ

Paul begins with the assertion, "I have been crucified with Christ." The core of the gospel is that Jesus came from heaven to bear in His death on the cross the full penalty that each of us deserves. The Perfect One died for the imperfect ones, a death the Father accepted as full atonement for sin.

But Paul says that in some way he himself participated in the Lord's crucifixion to the extent that he no longer lived. What does that mean? Not of course that he died physically with Christ. Rather,

Paul is speaking from the standpoint of his spiritual union with Jesus. Positioned in Christ when Christ died, the old Paul was also put to death. The cross delivered a fatal blow to his sinful self.

The principle at work here is *identification*. Paul so identified with Christ in His death that his old life was as good as dead. Whether Paul entered into this truth in Damascus at the time of his conversion or later in the desert we do not know. But by the time he wrote to the Galatians, he knew it to be true.

To our benefit, the Holy Spirit led Paul to enlarge upon this principle elsewhere in his Letters, most fully in Romans 6-8. He shows that identification with Christ in His death is absolutely essential for righteous living.

The reason is clear. We are not simply guilty of a few faults. By nature we are slaves to sin (Romans 6:6). Furthermore, Romans 7 makes it plain that all our efforts to liberate ourselves from this bondage are bound to fail. We can no more escape sin's crushing power than the prisoner can break free from ball and chain.

What *Can* Set Us Free?

How, then, can we be set free from the shackles of sin? Self-help seminars won't do it, or psychological reconditioning, or more self-discipline. Paul says the *only* remedy is for the "old man" to be put to death! (Romans 6:6, 11).

Death is the only way to destroy the power of the flesh. And the good news is that the old self *did* die, not physically on the cross, but by connection (identification) with Christ in *His* death. Paul asserts, "count yourselves dead to sin" (6:11).

Paul does not call reborn persons to a life-long standoff with the flesh. He says we are to consider ourselves dead and buried with Christ. Then we will "no longer be slaves to sin—because anyone who has died has been freed from sin" (6:6-7).

Any more I don't hear much teaching or preaching on identification with Christ in His death. Is it that contemporary Christians choose to seek the benefits of the gospel without the consequences of the cross? Could it be that pastors fear attendance will decline if they preach the truth about sin and sanctification to self-absorbed North Americans? Whatever the reasons, the silence is deadly. It robs the church of much-needed truth.

In reality the principle of identification with Christ's death produces new life! What could be better news than that? I long to see that truth recovered.

Possession by Christ

Paul moves on to testify that the death of his old self left no vacuum within. "I no longer live, but Christ lives in me." He no longer lived, for he was dead with Christ. But Paul really came alive because Christ lived out His life through him.

I have encountered a subtle fear among Christians. They think if they consider themselves dead to sin, their existence will be harsh, devoid of satisfaction and fulfillment. That fear circulates among Christians of all ages, not only the young.

But Paul's own experience is a powerful blow to this myth. Paul lived one of the most interesting lives history has ever recorded. There is nothing dull about shipwrecks, singing duets in jail at midnight, being let down a city wall in a basket—not to mention the thrill of being instrumental in the conversion and discipling of countless people.

Such fullness of life was the result of a second principle: *possession* by Christ. Any possible void in Paul's life was filled up with the life of the risen Christ within him. He did not merely revere a departed hero. He was united with and possessed by a living Lord who had risen from the dead.

That all believers are united with Christ in His resurrection is the declaration of Romans 6:4-5:

> *Just as Christ was raised from the dead through the glory of the Father, we too may live a new life.*
> *If we have been united with him like this in his death, we will certainly also be united with him in his resurrection.*

Though there is a reference to the final resurrection that we who are believers will share in, even now we are to count ourselves "alive to God in Christ Jesus" (6:11).

Identification with Christ in His death breaks the grip of the flesh. But the power for holy living flows from His resurrection into the lives of those He possesses. With such power, how can any believer go on sinning?

Appropriation of Christ

The risen Christ does not cheerlead our efforts at self-perfection. These are futile. Rather, He takes possession so that we may consider ourselves alive in Him. Counting this true opens up the tremendous prospect of holy living. More even than we desire it for ourselves, He desires to live out His triumph over sin in our lives.

The last sentence of Galatians 2:20 is the capstone of Paul's testimony: "The life I live in the body, I live by faith in the Son of God, who loved me and gave himself for me."

Although Paul did not witness Christ's ascension, it was revealed to him that the Father set His Son Jesus in the highest place and gave Him a name above every name (see Philippians 2:9). By virtue of His exaltation, Jesus gained the prerogative to reign over heaven and earth. He also gained full authority to empower His church (Matthew 28:18-19).

If all power resided in Christ and Paul was united with Him, then Christ's power was available to Paul by faith. Paul could say that though he was very much alive, he conducted his life and ministry by faith in Jesus Christ.

Here is the principle of *appropriation* at work. Paul took by faith what Christ provided to carry out the calling upon his life. Did he lack physical strength? He drew it from Christ. Did he lack the ability to persuade unbelievers to receive the gospel? He relied on Christ to convince them.

Did he need authority to invade spiritual darkness with the light of truth? Then he drew it from Christ. Did he need wisdom, discernment, perseverance, encouragement or anything else to complete his course? If so, he appropriated it from Christ by faith.

We Must Live by Faith

If there is a secret to a life of deepening holiness,

it is that we must live it by faith in Christ. There needs to be a beginning point. But what is begun must continue by appropriation of the risen Christ's victory, power and righteousness.

Paul knew that secret, and so he charged the Colossians:

> *Since, then, you have been raised with Christ, set your hearts on things above, where Christ is seated at the right hand of God. . . . Put to death . . . whatever belongs to your earthly nature: sexual immorality, impurity, lust, evil desires and greed, which is idolatry.* (Colossians 3:1, 5)

Those words speak to the church today with as much authority as when they were first written. They convince us that the only way to overcome our internal enemy, the flesh, is to consider ourselves to participate with Christ in His death, burial and resurrection.

Paul never attributed the supernatural results of his apostolate to his own gifts and intelligence. He drew upon Christ's unfailing resources to do the will of God. All his accomplishments for God were achieved that way.

It would not stretch the truth to say that the ministry of Paul in actuality was the ministry of Christ in and through him by the Holy Spirit.

Spiritual union with Christ at the very moment of salvation is the basis of our sanctification. Holiness is centered in Christ. As we recognize our identification with Him in His death and resurrection, as we allow Him to possess us, as we appropriate His available power, a holy life becomes possible.

Christ *is* our holiness.

Perspectives
on
Holiness

CHAPTER	Holiness
14	and the Conscience

by Paul F. Bubna

A S WE WERE SINGING THE closing hymn, I saw him leave his seat near the back of the sanctuary. He made his way slowly down the center aisle. I could see the tears on his cheeks. After the benediction, I knelt beside him.

Bill (not his real name) had been a believer since childhood. His faith was planted firmly in the saving work of Christ. But he described his daily walk as "a round of defeats." Day after day his conscience condemned him. Bill longed to live a holy life. He understood that the Holy Spirit had power to conform him to Christ's image. But in the face of this unabated inner condemnation, an intimate fellowship with God seemed impossible. Some days Bill was tempted to give up.

Exactly what is this thing we call conscience? Can we trust it? What do the Scriptures say about it? How does it relate to holy living?

What Is the Conscience?

Secular psychologists have explored the mystery

of the conscience and come to a variety of conclusions. Freud believed that we are born without a conscience and have no means of reality testing. Guilt feelings are conditioned by the demands and attitudes of our parents.

Fromm's view of conscience was more positive. He held that our conscience is developed mainly during the first few years of our life. He viewed conscience not merely as motivating us to avoid the pain of guilt and rejection but also to act for the good of others.

Mowrer and Glasser took yet another tack. They saw the conscience as a positive element in our human personality. Guilt feelings are to be taken seriously, with the answer lying in forgiveness and correct behavior.

Bruce Narramore, a Christian psychologist, in his book *No Condemnation,* suggests that a way to think about conscience that reflects Bible revelation is to see it as a series of processes. These processes are an expression of our moral nature. They are part of what it means to be created in the image of God.

Although Adam and Eve, Narramore says, were created as moral creatures in God's image, they likely did not experience conscience as we do. In the Garden of Eden they walked in perfect obedience and unbroken intimacy with God. We cannot imagine what it would be like to have our moral nature in perfect harmony with God's will and purpose.

When Adam and Eve fell into sin, within their moral nature the processes that we experience as conscience began to operate. For the first time they began to feel the pangs of guilt. They lost intimacy on every level. Adam and Eve hid themselves.

An Unreliable Indicator

Everything good about humankind was devastated by the Fall. Our moral nature—our conscience—was no exception. That inner voice is still there to urge obedience and to inflict the pain of guilt. But as an indicator of what is good or what is evil, it is not reliable. Those who program our conscience (parents, teachers, peers) are also fallen people. They suffer the same moral blindness we do.

In the worship of ancient Israel, the congregation in the desert was confronted with the awesome presence of the Lord God, but at the same time God was teaching them to "distinguish between the holy and the common, between the unclean and the clean" (Leviticus 10:10).

For 430 years Israel had been in Egypt. After generations of idol influence, these pilgrims needed their consciences trained in regard to the holy and the profane. Without this reprogramming their consciences would not be reliable.

The New Testament, too, points out the unreliability of the fallen conscience. The writer to the Hebrews chides his readers and hearers for their lack of spiritual growth:

> *Anyone who lives on milk, being still an infant, is not acquainted with the teaching about righteousness. But solid food is for the mature, who by constant use have trained themselves to distinguish good from evil.* (Hebrews 5:13-14)

The writer sees as a mark of maturity the ability to

distinguish good from evil. He asserts that people living on "milk" cannot fully understand the issue of righteousness. A biblically informed conscience is essential to holy living.

Dangerous Assumptions

Ask the average Christian to define the conscience and he or she will say it is the voice within us that tells us what is right or wrong. It affirms our right choices and makes us feel guilty about our wrong ones.

We tend to assume the conscience is some sort of a separate entity within us, a gift from God given to humankind at creation. It survived the Fall unscathed and still is operative within each of us.

On the surface these assumptions seem to fit our experience as believers. At the least, they appear to be harmless. In fact, these assumptions are not only false but dangerous. Let's go back to Bill's situation. If the voice inside Bill condemning him is God's gift, then God is condemning Bill. But the Word declares: "Therefore, there is now no condemmnation for those who are in Christ Jesus" (Romans 8:1).

Conscience has nothing to do with our standing before God. In response to repentance and saving faith, a great transaction has taken place within each Christian. "God made him who had no sin to be sin for us, so that in him we might become the righteousness of God" (2 Corinthians 5:21).

Our moral debt was placed on Christ, who in His death bore our sins. Christ's perfect righteousness has been put to our account. In God's eyes we stand spotless and pure. Whether our conscience agrees or not, this is fact, based on what God has done and not on human effort.

A Vital Factor in Holy Living

Conscience has nothing to do with our standing in Christ Jesus. It is, however, a vital factor in holy living. When we were born again, the Holy Spirit took up residence in us. Listen to how the apostle Paul describes the transforming power of the Holy Spirit in us:

> And we, who with unveiled faces all reflect the Lord's glory, are being transformed into his likeness with ever-increasing glory, which comes from the Lord, who is the Spirit. (2 Corinthians 3:18)

That transforming work is by God's grace and power. But how holy it makes us involves our response. From the human perspective, faith and submission to God are what holy living is all about. And a clear conscience is a key element in this response to God. Conversely, a condemning conscience will destroy the vitality of our trust in God's love and power.

We would like to think that Bill is an anomaly in the church. In reality, there are many Bills in most congregations.

Bill is in Christ Jesus. As a believer, if he sins he should expect feelings of guilt that prompt him to repent. But since Bill is in Christ Jesus, there can be no condemnation. The voice that condemns him is not telling the truth. Clearly we need a true-to-the-Scriptures understanding of conscience that explains Bill's predicament.

Three Pictures of the Conscience

The Greek word *suneidesis,* translated conscience in the New Testament, appears 31 times, all of them in the Letters, mostly Paul's. The root word carries the idea of self-awareness or a shared knowledge. In the New Testament the term implies the God-given ability for self-knowledge—being able to evaluate one's thoughts and actions over against a measuring stick.

It is possible for this conscience to be *seared,* no longer capable of sensing right from wrong. Paul warns about the "later times [when] some will abandon the faith and follow deceiving spirits and things taught by demons" (1 Timothy 4:1). "Such teachings," he says, "come through hypocritical liars, whose consciences have been seared as with a hot iron" (4:2). When people knowingly choose darkness instead of light, the day will come when the inner light of conscience is extinguished.

One of the fearful things of our time is to see young criminals who commit incredible acts of violence with seemingly no sense of guilt. The loss of conscience is an awful darkness.

The New Testament also pictures the *weak* conscience. Three times in First Corinthians 8, Paul uses the term, each time in the context of eating meat that has been offered to idols. Paul reasons that since an idol is nothing and there is only one God, the meat offered to idols is unaffected. There is no reason it cannot be eaten with thanksgiving. But he says some people's consciences are weak:

Some people are still so accustomed to idols that

*when they eat such food they think of it as having
been sacrificed to an idol, and since their conscience is weak, it is defiled.* (1 Corinthians 8:7)

Paul speaks of people whose consciences are
giving them false information. They feel guilty
about something in which they could have liberty
in Christ. But don't overlook Paul's concern "that
the exercise of your freedom does not become a
stumbling block to the weak" (8:9).

A Good Conscience

Paul knew what it was to face criticism. But he
was confident in his own integrity. Paul's ability to
keep his balance amid a barrage of criticism was
directly related to his carefulness to keep a good
conscience. He reminded Timothy that the whole
objective of his ministry should be "love, which
comes from a pure heart and a good conscience and
a sincere faith" (1 Timothy 1:5).

John Wesley taught that the essence of holiness is
love. Jesus told the young lawyer that loving God
totally is the greatest commandment. God's kind of
love is about obedience. It flows from a pure
heart—a heart intent on pleasing God supremely.
Purity of heart, says Paul, is enabled by a good conscience. And a good conscience is rooted in sincere
faith.

What is a good conscience? First, a good conscience has been liberated by saving faith. The burden of guilt has been lifted! We have been set free!
A good conscience is rooted in a faith that abides in
grace.

Second, a good conscience has a growing sensitivity to good and evil. This comes by meditating upon the Scriptures and integrating them into daily practice. What a joy it is when the voice of condemnation has been put to rest by bedrock trust in God's grace and the daily enlightenment of biblical truth!

Third, a good conscience has been kept lively by careful obedience. Paul tells Timothy: "Fight the good fight, holding on to faith and a good conscience" (1 Timothy 1:18-19). Our faith is not just an intellectual issue. It is a moral issue as well. Truth is not something we believe rationally. It must be fleshed out in holy living. Therefore, a good conscience is vital to our faith.

How Do We Keep a Good Conscience?

How do we keep a good conscience? By obedience. We hold on to faith. Faith is obeying what God tells us. The inner voice of conscience must not only be informed by the Scriptures, but they and it must be meticulously obeyed. God's mighty work of conforming our inner person to Christ-likeness involves daily obedience to God and to conscience. The crucial issues are matters of the heart—its desires, its passions, its attitudes and inner responses. It is there that the work of holiness is done. It is God's work, true. But He works when we yield our hearts to Him. "Trust and obey." "Faith and a good conscience."

The secret to a good conscience is not perfection but integrity—inner honesty about our condition. It would be glorious if we never violated our sense of right and wrong. The fact is we do. It is what we do at that point that is crucial to the pursuit of holy living. Some are overwhelmed by a sense of failure and choose to wallow in defeat, perhaps allowing their conscience to condemn them. Others endeavor to silence the voice of conscience by busyness—closing off the inner life.

The answer is to keep short accounts with God. John points the way to a good conscience. He calls it walking in the light:

> If we walk in the light, as he is in the light, we have fellowship with one another, and the blood of Jesus, his Son, purifies us from all sin.
>
> If we claim to be without sin, we deceive ourselves and the truth is not in us. If we confess our sins, he is faithful and just and will forgive us our sins and purify us from all unrighteousness. (1 John 1:7-9)

Many dear people live in spiritual stagnation simply because they are not careful about their consciences. It is God who works in us to conform us to Christ. But that good work cannot be done if we have shut the door to our inner life, endeavoring to ignore a guilty conscience. We must set our hearts to keep short accounts with God.

To do so will also mean keeping short accounts with people. Most often our sins bring pain to others. Harsh words. Selfishness. Lying. Broken promises. Failure to love. As we confess these failures to God, He most likely will call us to make things right with the person or persons we have wronged. If at this call to humility and confession we turn away, choosing to live instead with a defiled conscience, we shut the door to spiritual growth.

Conclusion

Years ago I set my heart to cultivate an inner fellowship with Christ. While I discipline myself to structured devotional times, my goal is to cultivate a life-style of continual inner fellowship with Christ. It is a blessed walk, but it has a cost. It demands complete and immediate obedience to the voice of conscience. And when I fail to obey, it calls for confession and cleansing. And frequently it calls for me to humble myself and seek forgiveness from others.

I cannot say that this pursuit is without discomfort. But the alternative—to close the door to my inner life and the pursuit of moment-by-moment fellowship with my Lord—is an unthinkable thought.

We began by affirming that our conscience has nothing to do with our standing before God. When we believe savingly upon Christ, we stand righteous before God, whether our conscience agrees or not. But a good conscience is essential to spiritual growth. John in his first Letter (3:19-22) summarizes it best:

> *This then is how we know that we belong to the truth, and how we set our hearts at rest in his presence whenever our hearts condemn us. For God is greater than our hearts, and he knows everything.*
>
> *Dear friends, if our hearts do not condemn us, we have confidence before God and receive from him anything we ask, because we obey his commands and do what pleases him.*

CHAPTER	A
15	Holy Man of God

by Fred S. Jennings

SHORTLY AFTER MIDNIGHT, JULY 30, 1964, I knelt in the family room of my house and asked God for help. I was a spiritual illiterate. I wasn't even sure if there *was* a God. I didn't know how to pray, and I didn't know if I would get an answer. But I told God if He existed I wanted to find Him.

Instantly, something shot out of my heart, raced across my mind and informed me that whatever I had been seeking I had just found! I was stunned. Something definite had just happened to me.

At once I went searching for a Bible and finally found one in a drawer of my dresser. I opened it at random—to Psalm 51. As I read David's confession of sin, I knew I was reading something written for me. God spoke to me through His Word. At last I had found Him.

Although I had started to read the Bible, I was still too ignorant spiritually to comprehend what had happened. Some time before that, I had met the pastor of a local church. I had no idea what he or his church believed. But I was in need of answers. With great reluctance, I took my questions to him.

My Two Questions

First, I asked the pastor to explain what had happened to me that night in my home. Briefly I reviewed the details for him.

"It sounds like you have been 'born again,' " he replied, quoting Jesus' words to Nicodemus from John 3:3. His answer made absolutely no sense to me, but I proceeded with a follow-up question.

"How can I stay 'born again'?" I asked. This time his reply seemed more ridiculous than before. He told me I should "pray continually" (1 Thessalonians 5:17).

I left our meeting convinced the pastor needed help worse than I did! Everything he said sounded absurd to me. I was to learn, however, that he had told me the truth.

I was disappointed because nothing the pastor said had appealed to my intellect. Wasn't I a college graduate, a former Air Force flying officer, the president of a family business? I deserved answers more sophisticated than what he had given me.

I had no awareness then that I was coming to grips with my natural mind that for years and years had been blinded by one called "the god of this world" (2 Corinthians 4:4). No wonder spiritual truth seemed foolish! My intellectual world compared natural things with what was natural. But God is Spirit (John 4:24). The new world that I had entered expressed "spiritual truths in spiritual words" (1 Corinthians 2:13). Only God's Holy Spirit could communicate the things of God to my spirit.

My Marriage Collapses

Within a short period of time my marriage collapsed—a direct result of my new commitment to Christ. It was the deepest inner wound I had ever experienced. Throughout that whole devastating time, my only guide was the Word of God. As I read the Word, it brought a sense of relief to my aching heart. I began to understand that what had happened to me the night I asked Jesus into my life wasn't psychological or intellectual. The relief and comfort I was beginning to experience wasn't just in my mind. I was mentally aware of the pain, but my awareness of this all-consuming sorrow was focused in my broken heart (Proverbs 15:13).

The conclusion of my marriage was swift. My wife received custody of our three-year-old daughter. I received custody of our eight-year-old son. As I watched the fabric of family life unravel, pain turned to inner rage. By the time of the actual divorce, I was consumed with anger. But then I read the words of Jesus: "I tell you: Love your enemies and pray for those who persecute you" (Matthew 5:44). The Holy Spirit used those words to pierce my heart.

My mind seemed to enter into an overwhelming battle. "A great contest in the face of suffering" (Hebrews 10:32) warred within me. My natural emotions fought against the truth that the Holy Spirit had spoken. To love an enemy was not in my nature. I began to question my motives. What I read in the Bible contradicted how I felt. The Holy Spirit had established residence in my heart, but a multitude of enemies were there to resist Him.

A Literal Holy War

I began to survey these enemies in what was becoming a literal holy war. As they struggled to the surface, I identified anger, hatred, resentment, bitterness. That night of July 30 when I crossed the bridge into the arms of Jesus, these fierce warriors accompanied me. Instantly, however, love, joy, peace and patience were there to launch a counterattack.

Gradually I began to realize that I was not born with the love of Christ. My human love was emotional. It was a self-serving love that fed on its own satisfaction. It prospered the most when its personal desires were gratified. The love of Christ was a contradiction to human love. It blossomed as it confronted the rejection of someone very dear and close.

At last I had identified the enemy, and it wasn't my wife. *My own human nature* was the enemy of God. It had to be brought into subjection. My nature had to be broken before God's love could be "poured out" into my heart "by the Holy Spirit" (Romans 5:5).

The night I received the Lord Jesus Christ into my life I passed from death to life. That night I was born again. But the process of becoming a holy man of God would span the rest of my life. From the moment I was born again, the Holy Spirit began his work of conforming me to the image of God's Son (Romans 8:29). I began to be fashioned into the image of "Jesus Christ, the Righteous One" (1 John 2:1). The Holy Spirit sought to create in me a mind that would think like Jesus (Philippians 2:5).

The Bible says, "We are God's workmanship, created in Christ Jesus to do good works, which God prepared in advance for us to do" (Ephesians 2:10).

A Second Important Event

The night of July 30 when I received Christ into my life was the night I passed from death to life. It was the night I was born again. But a second event was nearly as significant.

I began attending a church, and I began to hear messages about the person of the Holy Spirit. Subjects like holiness or being filled with the Spirit were foreign to me. When the pastor preached on sanctification, I didn't even know what the right questions were. But as he faithfully preached the message, I began to comprehend.

At that time, a layman whom God sent to help me mentioned being "filled with the Spirit." The words captured my attention because I began to sense a deep thirsting in my soul. The faithfulness of that pastor and that layman quickened my desire for a deeper sense of God's presence.

The final prompt was a statement of Jesus that I found in the New Testament: "If you then, though you are evil, know how to give good gifts to your children, how much more will your Father in heaven give the Holy Spirit to those who ask him!" (Luke 11:13). The words seemed clear enough, but I didn't know how to ask!

I knew I must find someone to help me, but I was too embarrassed to make inquiry. Finally I decided to visit another pastor whom I greatly respected. I drove to his office and he warmly received me. I presented him with my question about how to be filled with the Spirit. He urged me simply to ask the Holy Spirit by faith to fill me. I did as he directed. It was May 12, 1972.

No Feeling

I felt nothing. Within a few days, the significance of the event drifted from my mind. But before long the Holy Spirit would bring it to my remembrance. It was about a month after my praying to be filled with the Holy Spirit that I sensed a disturbance within me, a deep emptiness permeating my heart. At first, I didn't associate it with my asking for the Holy Spirit.

I began to recall acts of dishonesty from my past. Some of them frightened me, but I determined to make them right. The Holy Spirit went through my business. He had me make right every act of dishonesty (2 Corinthians 4:1-2). I returned to my college and made restitution for other acts of dishonesty. I had to terminate a business relationship with an unsaved partner (2 Corinthians 6:14-18). I reimbursed overtime to employees whom in earlier years I had shortchanged (James 5:4). To "renounce [these] secret and shameful ways" (2 Corinthians 4:2), I had to sell a building that had been providing me a very substantial profit.

God's Spirit led me to Hebrews 5:8-9: "Although he was a son, he learned obedience from what he suffered and, once made perfect, he became the source of eternal salvation for all who obey him." I was learning obedience and, at the same time, being cleansed from past sin. This had nothing to do with my salvation, but it had everything to do with my sanctification. The Lord was emptying me and cleansing me of all those things that had accumulated in the years prior to my salvation. The process took 10 days, but at the end of that time sin took on a new meaning. God brought me very low before I sensed the return of His peace and assurance.

My Thoughts, Too

As I began to ponder my thought life, I was amazed to discover that I no longer entertained sin in my mind. Lascivious and evil thoughts still coursed through my mind, but they no longer took up residence. I knew that the battle with sin raged in my mind, but I never knew that my imagination and thoughts could be harnessed. I discovered a new discipline that seemed to govern my inner person. It was as if the Holy Spirit was ushering out every evil thought. In His day-by-day renewing power, the Holy Spirit was taking "captive every thought to make it obedient to Christ" (2 Corinthians 10:5).

The process of becoming a holy man is a living experience. Both salvation and the filling of the Spirit are imperative to it. Only as every recess of a man's heart is filled with the Holy Spirit can he live a holy life. Jesus said, "The Spirit gives life; the flesh counts for nothing. The words I have spoken to you are spirit and they are life" (John 6:63). As we develop spiritually, God separates us from the world and transforms us into the image of Jesus Christ with ever-increasing glory (see 2 Corinthians 3:18).

"Therefore let us leave the elementary teachings about Christ and go on to maturity, not laying again the foundation of repentance from acts that lead to death, and of faith in God" (Hebrews 6:1). As I left the dead works of my human, sinful nature, I experienced the power of God through the infilling of His Holy Spirit. I encountered a new plateau in my spiritual pilgrimage.

The Word of God sets forth God's clear command: "Be holy, because I am holy" (1 Peter 1:16). I discovered that as the process moved forward, it was not simply a matter of a Spirit-controlled life; it also resulted in a Spirit-empowered life.

Triumph!

It was a beautiful day in late August, 1993. My son was getting married, and the wedding would be in my house. His mother attended, sitting on the front row with her husband. It had been 29 years since our divorce. I had last seen her at the marriage of our daughter in 1984. As I looked at her across the room, I could sincerely praise God who had crushed me with an instrument only He could select. I was no longer bound in the chains of resentment and bitterness.

The Holy Spirit long since had killed my human love, replacing it with a flow of divine love that only He could give. God had "poured out his love into [my heart] by the Holy Spirit, whom he [had] given [me]" (Romans 5:5).

When the ceremony was concluded, my son asked me to pray for him and his bride. As I went forward, I was able to pray a blessing upon the mother who had given us such a lovely daughter-in-law, and *a blessing upon the mother who had given us such a fine son*. The events of that day demonstrated to me the power of God in holy conduct.

What might have been for me a wretched day was instead a day of great blessing and victory. Thirty years had passed since my first faltering word of prayer to a God I was not even sure existed. That night Jesus had entered my life. Thirty years later, on my son's wedding day, God arranged a mid-term exam. It was God's testing time for what the Holy Spirit had brought about in me. I suspect it was more for my benefit than His, except that He receives all the glory! In every area, God had preserved me.

As I watched my son's mother follow the bride and groom to a waiting car, a phrase of Scripture flashed across my mind: "[A pearl] of great value" (Matthew 13:45-46). How thankful I was that God had laid upon my heart her soul at any cost. I was confident that the time would come when He would reconcile her to Himself. God was working His purpose. Sensing His love, I began to understand His freedom.

Jesus said, "If the Son sets you free, you will be free indeed" (John 8:36). I was a free man.

A Holy Man of God

Paul prayed this way for the Thessalonian believers: "May [the Lord] strengthen your hearts so that you will be blameless and holy in the presence of our God and Father when our Lord Jesus comes with all his holy ones" (1 Thessalonians 3:13). Holiness is not a human virtue. But in Christ it is an ongoing metamorphosis as "we, who with unveiled faces all reflect the Lord's glory, are being transformed into his likeness with ever-increasing glory, which comes from the Lord, who is the Spirit" (2 Corinthians 3:18).

The ultimate conclusion for a holy man is sonship. "Now we are children of God, and what we will be has not yet been made known. But we know that when he appears, we shall be like him, for we shall see him as he is" (1 John 3:2). When the Holy Spirit has produced a holy spirit within a man, His completed work is a son who thinks like his Father. When that happens, we have a holy man of God.

Sanctification is divine holiness, not human self-improvement or perfection. It is the inflow into our being of the life and purity of God's own perfection and the working out of His own will. We remain as insignificant and insufficient as ever. It is the Person who dwells within us who possesses and exercises all the gifts and powers of our ministry. As we abide in Him and He works in us we are able to exercise this power.
—A.B. Simpson—

Holy Women of God

by Charlotte Stemple

IF YOU ARE LIKE ME, the term *holy women* brings to mind historical figures we've read about: Madame Guyon, Amy Carmichael, Rosalind Goforth, Hannah Whitall Smith. But are all the holy women confined to history books? What would a holy woman look like today?

Are all holy women contemplative and mystical? Are at least some of them practical as well as devotional? Is life in our fast-paced contemporary setting incompatible with holiness?

As I reflected on some of the women I know, God reassured me that His Spirit is still making people holy. Here are some things nine of them have taught me.

The First

She was a missionary in Vietnam at an exciting time. The war was at its wildest, but amid the chaos Christ was building His church. Missionaries were exhausted and tense as they gathered for their annual conference.

At that convocation God poured out His Spirit in genuine renewal. God gave new strength and joy for the spiritual warfare yet to come. To some He gave sign gifts.

She longed for a sign gift. Instead, God witnessed to her spirit in the words of Scripture: "Now I will show you the most excellent way. If I speak in the tongues of men and of angels, *but have not love,* I am only a resounding gong or a clanging cymbal" (1 Corinthians 12:31-13:1, emphasis added). God overwhelmed her heart to the bursting point with the gift of *love. For every ministry that followed, God's divine love sustained and motivated her.

The Holy Spirit graciously moved into the Vietnamese church in sweeping revival. Montagnard believers in the highlands also felt God's power and presence. The revival purified the church and prepared it for the enlarged harvest that followed. The Communist takeover of South Vietnam and the resulting restrictions on the church have not hampered its amazing growth.

When in 1975 Western personnel had to leave, this missionary, changed and changing by the Spirit's work, ministered from refugee camps to women's conferences, from hospitals to hurting homes, from Asia to North America. She is living evidence that "love never fails" (1 Corinthians 13:8).

She is a holy woman. I will call her *Love.*

The Second

She needed help. Once a vibrant Christian teenager, she now found life empty. Her marriage had failed, leaving strained relationships. She had an active son just entering adolescence.

Then God put in her heart a desire to be back on speaking terms with Him. So she packed a tent and drove to summer camp, hoping to meet God.

And meet Him she did! Kneeling at the altar for complete cleansing, she knew again the wholeness that is a specialty of our Redeemer God. The joy of the Lord filled her being and sent her home to make some necessary changes in her life-style and to reestablish patterns of spiritual growth.

Each of the next two or three summers she returned to camp. At the altar she underwent her "annual spiritual checkup," as she termed it. She was becoming a lovely holy woman of God.

Through a series of unlikely events, God orchestrated her life into a ministry beside a new husband at that same camp. Now she is known for her encouraging notes, her warm baked goods, her earnest praying for other wives in ministry. Staff and campers, adults, teens, children seek her company. All who know her think of her as a joy-bringer. Daily she finds ways to use her home and gifts for Jesus and for others.

She is a holy woman—a saint in sneakers! I will call her *Joy*.

The Third

Many full and fulfilling years of ministry were behind her and her pastor husband. They retired to a small house in our town, anticipating visits to children, other travel, relaxing hobbies.

And then she became ill—a rare, frightening illness for which there was no cure. Surgery after surgery has disfigured her face and left her barely able to talk. All her food intake must be liquids administered through a feeding tube.

It was a dramatic reversal of their retirement plans, but I never heard a bitter or complaining word. She writes:

"When physical problems could have made me anxious, I meditated on Philippians 4:6-7 ['Do not be anxious about anything. . . . The peace of God . . . will guard your hearts and your minds']. . . . This peace is the fruit of the Holy Spirit's life in me."

Refusing to be a recluse, she is church librarian and helps her husband with the active seniors group. She shops and visits and walks in her neighborhood. People recognize her by the cloth she holds over her lower face and the smile in her eyes.

She and I have a wonderful partnership. In my public ministry, I am her "mouth" and she is my "pray-er!" She knows my schedule and upholds me at the time of my ministry.

Their home is a haven of peace. People go there for counsel, encouragement, prayer. Every time I visit I am reminded that this is what seeing Christ's life in human circumstances looks like.

She is a holy woman. I will call her *Peace.*

The Fourth

Even as a teenager, she was tender to God and eager to obey Him. Inner beauty and strength matched outer beauty and capability—a rare combination in one so young. I can still see her walking across the Dalat School campus, books to her chin, but ready at a toss of her long hair to stop and talk. The daughter of missionaries, she sensed God's call to missions. College followed high school, and seminary, college. She was in seminary when the severe headaches began. Extensive tests revealed a pituitary tumor deep inside her head.

The surgery was not done well. Two years later a second surgery was necessary, with follow-up surgery two months after that. Determinedly, she kept at her seminary studies. She continued to excel in the classroom and in friendships. Then the symptoms returned and a fourth critical surgery was necessary. This one was followed by radiation to keep the unremovable part of the tumor from growing back. Once again she walked across a school campus with a stack of books, this time her head wrapped in a jaunty scarf until her beautiful hair would grow back.

Graduating finally, she found a place of service in a Midwestern church, where she serves as a highly effective woman in ministry.

Recently she turned "thirty-something," now fully accredited and under missionary appointment. Again she is waiting, this time for a visa into the country where she grew up. As I had opportunity recently to join her for a missions conference, I was amazed to recall the stops and starts of her long journey and to see her steadfast determination to serve God wherever she is.

From teenager to lovely young woman, she has been and is *a holy woman of God*. I will call her *Patience*.

The Fifth

As college students, my husband and I were offered a unique Christian service assignment. Would we be willing to go each weekend to a church two hours away to work with their youth? The church couldn't afford a full-time staff member. If we would go, they would cover travel costs. The pastor and his wife would see that we had a room and meals.

The first weekend I was nervous, but never again. The pastor and his wife welcomed us warmly. It was instant rapport. For nine months we shared their lives and home three days a week. She was absolutely consistent in her walk with the Lord, her love for their congregation and her servant heart.

Each weekend I found our room spotlessly clean with a special welcome waiting for us. She had planned and prepared the meals ahead so we could use our time to visit the youth. She helped us track down addresses and prepare for youth activities.

She was the church musician. By the time we arrived, she had practiced for Sunday. Her life was dedicated with joy to her husband's ministry and, by extension, to us. I knew we were pampered and praised; I didn't realize we were being taught and trained.

Every weekend was filled with "random acts of kindness"—and not just for us. Each member of the congregation knew her loving heart and hand. To me she epitomizes so many ministry wives, consistent over the long haul with daily acts of mercy and love.

She is a holy woman. I will call her *Kindness.*

The Sixth

She could easily fit the description of Tabitha/Dorcas in Acts 9—except that she is still very

172

much alive. She is a saint with a sewing machine. At her own expense she has gone five times overseas to sew drapes and other necessary items at missionary installations.

She has infected her four children with a love for missions. For more than a year the whole family worked as the church's custodians to accrue money for a memorable trip to Ecuador to visit missionaries who had stayed in their home.

Recent financial difficulties have necessitated a very scaled-back, simple life-style for her and her husband. Instead of complaints, I have seen contentment and creativity. I have watched her "stretch" everything from food to space to bits of materials in order to keep up her lifelong habit of sharing what they have with others.

Her leadership skills have made her effective in local, district and national positions. She is very practical. For every plan or idea, she wants to concentrate on the "How to." She takes my frequently "flighty" ideas and makes them practical. How often she has brought me up short with the good journalism questions: Who? What? Why? Where? When? How?

She never seems too tired or too busy or too stressed to help those who need a room wallpapered, a cushion mended, a partner for prayer or someone to walk with. Her "works" attest to her deep love of the Lord and her relationship to Him.

She is a holy woman. I will call her *Goodness.*

The Seventh

I met her when I was teaching nurses at a

children's hospital in Danang, Vietnam—a hospital built and run by American military units. She was bright, vivacious, articulate and skilled. By trade she was a seamstress, but the Americans had taught her nursing. Her specialty was pediatric plastic surgery, which blended her seamstress skills and the medical art she had gained by carefully observing visiting American professionals.

Always on the move, she reminded me of a hummingbird drinking deeply but quickly at each encounter. Student nurses and her small patients alike loved her.

The Americans took her to the States to help raise money for the hospital. While there, a host family led her to Christ.

I did not know this. As I saw her each week, the Lord prodded me to invite her to study the Bible. I resisted, feeling she would be insulted if I inferred she had any spiritual need. She seemed always to have her life completely under control.

Finally I gave in. She responded with so much enthusiasm I was shocked. I have never met a person so hungry for God's Word, so impatient to learn, so eager to obey.

Soon she became active in the local church, especially the women's witness group. She led her family members to Christ.

Today she is active in the North American Vietnamese church. She has a wide ministry to the refugee community. I have watched her Christian life from newborn to maturity. Never have I seen her trust falter, even in unbelievable circumstances. Today she stands strong as a godly woman in her home and church.

She is a holy woman. I will call her *Faithfulness.*

The Eighth

She is no longer here, but she had a profound impact on my life at a very crucial time. And not only on mine, but on the lives of hundreds of young women who were under her guiding influence. She was Dean of Women at Nyack (New York) College.

While I was a student there, she had an apartment in the girls' dorm. Her door was always open. She invited small groups of girls to dinner each week until all had been in her home. It was an opportunity to observe her lovely table setting, to enjoy her simple, practical and delicious menu, to learn to hold easy, meaningful conversation with friends.

She was aware of each girl's personality and background. Her personal affirmation and trust enabled many of us to go much farther than we might otherwise have gone.

She was no "plastic saint" untouched by the realities of life. Her own missionary husband, after a short marriage, had died during World War II at the hands of the Japanese. He remained the great love of her life. At the end of the war she herself went to serve where he had died.

Effective as a missionary, she was now a mentor and model for young women preparing for life and ministry. More than 30 years later, I remember so many things about this woman and thank God she was a part of my life.

She was a holy woman. I will call her *Gentleness.*

The Ninth

For eight years she has been my prayer partner. I love her like a sister and know her even better.

Despite the difference in our ages, our families "connect" at many points. We have shared much laughter, some pain and plenty of questions.

She is an attractive young woman who laughs readily, a great conversationalist and fun to be around. She is well-educated, professionally employed, involved in church and school activities and committed to her husband and daughters.

The two of us prayed for God to be formed in us and our families, and we saw Him do some wonderful things. But all was not well inside this apparently "together" woman. As the emotional symptoms surfaced, stresses became irrational fears, competence became an unhealthy driven-ness.

As we battled in prayer through these unexpected agonies, my friend sensed the need for professional help in what would prove to be a long-term journey to wholeness. Through prayer and Christian counsel, she has learned to allow the Holy Spirit to confirm her worth in Christ. He is assuring her of the Father's love and acceptance. In her relationships with others, He is helping her to live without a mask.

As problems surface—and they still do—she has a base for decision-making that is healthy and holy. She is a Nineties woman, now neither co-dependent nor independent but God-dependent.

She is a holy woman. I will call her *Self-Control.*

Conclusion

These are some of my friends, and they represent many others.

Sometimes our thinking is very stereotyped. A missionary or a pastor's wife a holy woman? Well,

176

of course! But a divorcee, a teenager, one undergoing counseling, a refugee? At first thought, they don't fit our idea of holiness. But why not? When the theology of the Spirit of Christ as Helper, Comforter, Teacher and Counselor intersects with the particulars of our daily lives, the words *holy woman* take on new meaning.

These nine personal friends represent many others in whom I have seen the characteristics of *holy* forming. There is the professor's wife who tutors Muslim students and loves them so much she takes them along on their vacations. There is the pastor's wife who mentors her women in prayer. There is the single secretary who spends weekends visiting shut-ins, doing acts of kindness for them. There is my cousin who has poured her weekdays into the public school and her precious free time into her local church. There is my 80-year-old aunt who leads volunteers in a nursing home. And my friend who chooses not to work for wages but as a hospice volunteer. There are many more women of prayer and good deeds who know the reality of Jesus alive in them each day.

They can be described by the fruit of the Spirit they evidence and the gifts of the Spirit they use for Christ's body, the church. They are many. *I will call them holy women.*

CHAPTER	Holiness and
	the Mission-
17	ary Motive

by Wallace C.E. Albrecht

FROM THE FOUR CORNERS OF the globe, people make their way to Niagara Falls. They come by the millions to see the awesome beauty of this natural wonder. Newlyweds honeymoon at the Falls. Families include Niagara in their vacation plans. Indisputably, Niagara Falls is world-renowned for its imposing grandeur.

In similar fashion King David, enthralled by the awesome grandeur of God's holiness, issued a worldwide decree:

> *Worship the LORD in the splendor of his holiness;*
> *tremble before him, all the earth.*
> (Psalm 96:9)

David knew God firsthand. He knew the excellencies of the Almighty. Earnestly he desired every person on the face of the earth to "worship the Lord in the splendor of his holiness."

Therein lies the driving motivation for missions.

The splendor of God's majesty and the purity of His holiness stand in complete contrast to the hideous idols and seductive images before which so many of earth's people bow. Those who have traveled and seen these stark and distorted images—as I have—better understand that "the splendor of [the Lord's] holiness" *must* be exalted among the nations. God's holiness is the acme of purity, truth and perfection.

Holiness and Missions Are Inseparable

God revealed Himself personally to Abraham, Isaac and Jacob. He revealed Himself powerfully to Moses. He revealed Himself completely in the person of Jesus Christ. We who are truly acquainted with this God should have a compelling motivation to make Him known to all earth's peoples. John Piper in *Let the Nations Be Glad* has phrased it well:

> *The great sin . . . is not that the human race has failed to work for God so as to increase His glory, but that we have failed to delight in God so as to reflect His glory. . . . God's inexorable purpose to display His glory in the mission of the church is virtually the same as His purpose to give His people infinite delight. . . . God is committed to the holy joy of the redeemed, gathered from every tribe and tongue and people and nation, with the same zeal that moves Him to seek His own glory in all that He does.*

Frequently we express this inseparable relation between holiness and missions from a very human perspective. If God has done so much for us, delivering us from sin and qualifying us for heaven, should we not want to share this liberating news with everyone we encounter? How can we not earnestly desire that those who now are worshiping lesser gods come to a saving knowledge of the true and living God?

Holiness and missions, I repeat, are inseparable. The relationship is two-sided, like the two sides of a coin. It is two-sided because holiness has two sides. There is what I call the severe side and there is the beautiful side.

The Severe Side of Holiness

In the midst of Jesus Christ's Sermon on the Mount He stated God's will for humankind: "Be perfect, therefore, as your heavenly Father is perfect" (Matthew 5:48). God's standard is high. His expectation is nothing short of perfection.

Even by human standards, perfection is a stupendous challenge for mortals. Yet Jesus implies in the text just quoted that human standards of perfection are not sufficient. He expects—requires—us to rise to the perfection of God Himself. In fact, the Bible informs us that if we fall short of God's perfection, we are destined to separation from God.

"Without holiness no one will see the Lord" (Hebrews 12:14). This is the severe side of holiness. It should be a compelling motivation for missions. The good news amid the severity is that we do not have to rise to such a lofty standard by our own strength and resolve. The holiness that we need in order to see God is in the person of Jesus Christ Himself.

How beautifully that hope was celebrated by Zechariah, father of John the Baptist. Under the driving wind of God's Spirit Zechariah exulted:

Praise be to the Lord, the God of Israel,
   because he has come and has redeemed his
   people. . . .
   . . . to enable us to serve him without fear
in holiness and righteousness before him
   all our days. (Luke 1:68-75)

But what about those who have not heard this
good news? What about those who remain in darkness, worshiping their strange and capricious idols?
These who are steeped in vanity, corruption and
confusion—what hope have they?

The severe side of God's holiness is a powerful
missionary motive. Our compassion for people who
are captives of sin and in eternal danger should
compel us to see that they, too, have opportunity to
trust in Jesus Christ. To remain unconcerned about
the condition of those who have never heard is
criminal.

Indeed, that is exactly how God regards it. He told
Ezekiel very plainly, "When I say to a wicked man,
'You will surely die,' and you do not warn him or
speak out to dissuade him from his evil ways in
order to save his life, that wicked man will die for
his sin, and I will hold you accountable for his
blood" (Ezekiel 3:18).

The Beautiful Side of Holiness

To focus only on the severe side of God's holiness
and its inherent motivation for missionary work
would be analogous to coaxing the proverbial one-
winged bird to fly. We must behold the beautiful
side of God's holiness and note how it motivates us
to missions.

A great day is coming! In ignorance the nations wait for that day. Even creation itself groans for it to come. It will be a day when wrongs are made right, when inequities will be balanced, when offenses will be rectified, when perfection will reign.

A day is coming when a highway of holiness will encompass this world, restoring it to its intended purposes, making paradise a reality. Isaiah predicted it:

> Then will the eyes of the blind be opened
>   and the ears of the deaf unstopped.
> Then will the lame leap like a deer,
>   and the mute tongue shout for joy.
> Water will gush forth in the wilderness
>   and streams in the desert. . . .
>
> And a highway will be there;
>   it will be called the Way of Holiness.
> The unclean will not journey on it;
>   it will be for those who walk in that Way. . . .
> Only the redeemed will walk there,
>   and the ransomed of the LORD will return.
> They will enter Zion with singing;
>   everlasting joy will crown their heads.
> Gladness and joy will overtake them,
>   and sorrow and sighing will flee away.
>   (Isaiah 35:5-10)

The Way of Holiness is the goal toward which we are moving! It should motivate us to guarantee that every man, woman, youth and child on the face of the earth in every generation has the opportunity to choose this road.

It is a road that will run from Baghdad through

Jerusalem all the way to Cairo. Isaiah goes on to say:

> In that day there will be a highway from Egypt to Assyria. The Assyrians will go to Egypt and the Egyptians to Assyria. The Egyptians and Assyrians will worship together. In that day Israel will be the third, along with Egypt and Assyria, a blessing on the earth. The LORD Almighty will bless them, saying, "Blessed be Egypt my people, Assyria my handiwork, and Israel my inheritance." (Isaiah 19:23-25)

Dare we speculate that this highway may also run through Libya and Algeria, Morocco and Mauritania including the now trenchant Muslim populations of those nations? Will it go on down to Conakry, Abidjan, Lagos and Libreville, where missionaries today are bringing in a bountiful harvest? Will it stretch elsewhere to band together South Africa and Europe, Asia and the Pacific islands, our Western Hemisphere? I believe we can expect that. Why? Because our Holy God is also a missionary God!

A Holy God, a Missionary God

Holiness and missions are inseparable because our Holy God is a missionary God. His vision, His passion, His purposes encompass all people and all nations. God's worldwide love, inscribed in Holy Writ from Genesis through Revelation, needs to be inscribed as well on our hearts.

From the first intimation of a serpent-defeating Messiah (Genesis 3:15) to Revelation's glimpses of that great heavenly congregation of overcomers singing praise to God (7:9-12, 19:1-8), the nations of earth are front-and-center in God's master plan. Again, Israel's poet-king writes:

> Ascribe to the LORD, O families of nations,
>   ascribe to the LORD glory and strength.
> Ascribe to the LORD the glory due his name;
>   bring an offering and come into his courts.
> (Psalm 96:7-8)

The prophet Ezekiel likewise underscores God's emphasis on nations:

> I will show my greatness and my holiness, and I will make myself known in the sight of many nations. Then they will know that I am the LORD."
> (Ezekiel 38:23)

God is determined to make Himself known, to display the glory of His holiness in every nation and among every ethnic group in our world. To work in harmony with God is to adopt His agenda for the world.

Jesus declared while He was on earth, "Whatever the Father does the Son also does" (John 5:19). He also said, "As the Father has sent me, I am sending you" (John 20:21). We are commissioned by Jesus to do what we see the Father doing. And without doubt our Father God is determined to reveal the glory of His holiness to the peoples of our world. This, then, should be our task as well.

The goal, as Piper states it, is "to bring the nations into the white-hot enjoyment of God's glory. The goal of missions is the gladness of the peoples in the greatness of God."

Missions Is a Motivation to Holiness

Even as holiness is a motivation to missions, so missions is a motivation to holiness. Missions in today's world demands a standard of practical holiness that will attract the attention of people who are very cynical about the "Christian West." *We* differentiate between Bible-believing, born-again followers of Christ and those held captive by the prevailing North American secular humanism. Most people in other nations do not. For many, the only concept of *Christian* comes through the filthy grade B movies that Hollywood readily distributes worldwide. Little wonder that the Muslim world in particular is turned off by our decadence. Only as they see holiness personified in us will they begin to understand.

Aziz, a young man living with his parents in a Muslim nation, had a dream. In his dream he saw a little blond boy approach the house where he lived. In Aziz's dream, the boy told Aziz that his family would be moving in across the street and that his daddy had most wonderful news for him.

Sure enough, several weeks later a "tent-making" missionary family moved into the house across the street. Aziz immediately recognized the little towheaded pre-schooler as the boy of his dream.

Aziz watched the family closely. He observed how well they got along together, their habits, their manner of living. They even *prayed*.

One day Aziz caught the foreigner coming out of his yard.

"Sir," said Aziz, "I've been watching you. You make a very good Muslim!"

The tentmaker smiled. "As a matter of fact, I am not a Muslim. I am a follower of Jesus Christ." He was careful to avoid the word *Christian*.

Aziz went on to tell him about his dream and how eager he was to hear the "most wonderful news" that the man's blond-headed son had promised.

God's sovereign intervention, coupled by the holy life of a tent-making missionary, brought Aziz to saving faith in Jesus Christ.

May God give His church in our day a host of holy servants so that His "ways may be known on earth," His "salvation among all nations."

How liberating it is to be wholly free by death from the entangling weight of our old habits, memories and the discouraging sense of our past! How great to spring, death-born, into a life of holiness and victory! It is our privilege.
—A.B. Simpson—

CHAPTER

18

False Holiness

by John A. Corby, Jr.

IT WAS SUNDAY MORNING WORSHIP in the fast-growing Avea Deux church in Libreville, Gabon. There must have been 3,000 people crowded into the building that day. Everyone was standing, arms outstretched toward heaven, eyes closed, faces raised, their bodies swaying to the music.

Amid that sea of people was a section of perhaps 20 children, ages 8-12. And those children were doing *exactly* as the adults around them. Their expressions were even more ecstatic, if possible, than those of the adults.

A jumble of thoughts ran through my mind. *Could these kids really know what church was all about? Did they understand what they were doing? Did they know what it means to truly worship God?*

After the service, I quizzed some of children.

"Do you know Jesus?" I asked.

"Oh, yes, and we love Him!" they chorused.

"Why do you come to church?"

"Because that's what Christians do."

"Why do you sing?"

"Because that's what Christians do!"

"Do you know *why* you raise your arms, close your eyes and lift your faces toward heaven?"

"Oh, yes! Because that's what Christians do!"

"But why do you do it? Do you know what *worship* is?"

"Worship? Well, that's what we do when we do all this. That is what Christians do!"

These young children were mimicking the adults. They believed their actions and words equated with Christianity. I did some more investigating and discovered than many of the new believers had the same impression: *I am a Christian because of what I do or say. If I act like the other believers in this church, then I am one.*

A Universal Problem

The phenomenon is not limited to Central Africa, where I ministered before my present assignment to France. Christians around the world—especially new Christians—may regard external signs as evidence of inner life and holiness. It's easier to adopt the form than to wait before God for the inner power.

Our society contributes to the problem. Do we not measure success in terms of outward achievement: wealth, life-style, social status? Christians become squeezed into the pressure mold of this world (see Romans 12:2). They are naturally inclined to want to measure holiness in the same way, by what a person does, says or achieves.

Jesus—in fact, all of the New Testament—teaches clearly that holiness is something internal. The true measure of holiness must be based on the inward changes achieved uniquely by the Holy Spirit.

The Scriptures liken us to sheep. A sheep's main weakness is that it *follows*. If there is no shepherd to lead it, a sheep follows all the other sheep in the flock. It does everything without reflection, without thinking. That can be dangerous.

In Gabon, I quickly learned to slow my truck whenever I saw a flock of sheep. Since there rarely were any shepherds, the sheep roamed freely. In spite of the sound of my approaching truck, or even its horn, sheep could bolt across the road in front of me at any moment and for no apparent reason. Those who ran first usually had no trouble making it across, but those who followed were always in mortal danger.

Look for a moment at Jesus' words in Matthew 7. In the context of the high ethical and moral standards He set forth in His Sermon on the Mount, Jesus speaks of false prophets who "come to you in sheep's clothing, but inwardly they are ferocious wolves" (7:15). They may *look* like sheep and even *act* like sheep (at first), but their single goal is to destroy and devour.

Fruit and False Prophets

Jesus goes on to say that you can determine whether a tree is good or bad by the fruit it produces. "A good tree cannot bear bad fruit, and a bad tree cannot bear good fruit" (7:18).

Why is Jesus talking about false prophets and fruit at the same time? Don't they seem to be incongruous?

Jesus brings the two disparate ideas together because He sees danger here. He explains: "Not everyone who says to me, 'Lord, Lord,' will enter the kingdom of heaven, but only he who does the will of my Father who is in heaven" (7:21).

But isn't that a contradiction of what Peter says, quoting the prophet Joel, as he addresses the crowd in Jerusalem at Pentecost? "Everyone who *calls* on the name of the Lord will be saved" (Acts 2:21, emphasis added).

No, it is not a contradiction. Peter's whole message to the crowd of startled, skeptical people was based on the necessity of *believing*, not just saying, that Jesus is both Lord and Christ.

What about the Bible's affirmation that "if you confess with your mouth, 'Jesus is Lord' . . . you will be saved" (Romans 10:9)? To be sure, the Bible says that, but do not overlook the rest of the verse: "If you confess with your mouth, 'Jesus is Lord,' *and believe in your heart* that God raised him from the dead, you will be saved" (emphasis added).

Salvation Involves the Heart

To be saved involves more than uttering the words "Jesus is Lord." Demons know that much, and they are already condemned. To be saved involves the heart. The heart, in biblical terms, is not merely the seat of the emotions and affections but also of the intellect and the will.

Heart belief involves a sense of remorse for our sins. We must then request forgiveness of God, who alone is able to forgive sin. In the process we must consciously, willfully receive Jesus Christ into our life as Lord. That is *conversion*—turning from our old self and our old way of life and following the One who gives new, eternal life. It involves, as I said, our intellect and our will. We can master the "Christianese" language, we can mimic "Christian" manners to perfection, we can follow the Christian prohibitions. But if we think by so doing we are Christians, we are mistaken.

Our world keeps insisting that the measure of a person's success is what he or she says, what he or she does. Jesus debunks that yardstick with these decisive words: "Many will say to me on that day, 'Lord, Lord, did we not prophesy in your name, and in your name drive out demons and perform many miracles?' Then I will tell them plainly, 'I never knew you. Away from me, you evildoers!' " (Matthew 7:22-23).

I fear that many people in our churches today believe themselves to be Christians based primarily on what they *say* (having heard other believers talk that same way) and on what they *do* (having seen other believers doing those things). These unthinking sheep are prime targets for the wolves since they accept everything based solely on appearance. It doesn't seem that we pay much attention to the dangers of the disguised wolves among us. We pay a lot of attention to what we look like and how we act. But I wonder if we are paying any attention to who and what we really are.

Head Scarf or "Sheep's Clothing"?

In discussing numerous problems within the congregation at Corinth, Paul instructs women to cover their heads when they pray or prophesy as "a sign of authority on her head" (1 Corinthians 11:10). Frequently this has been an issue among Gabonese Christians. Some churches have gone so far as to require all women attending church services to wear scarves on their heads. The reasoning was simple: "That's what the Bible says." At least, on the surface.

Those who wore scarves were accepted. Those who did not wear scarves were suspected of being insubordinate and thus not really Christians. But there was a problem. Women not living for the Lord and some who were still pagans came to church wearing scarves. And simply because they wore scarves, they were received as committed believers!

One day a young pastor approached me about this issue. In his church some known prostitutes had been attending the services, but not for pious reasons. Because they wore the scarves, they fit right in. Some in the congregation, however, knew they were prostitutes and knew why they were there.

"How," the pastor wanted to know, "can I reconcile the way these women *appear to be* with what they *really are*?"

I took the pastor back almost to the beginning of church history. In the early centuries, the Donatists insisted on a list of things that identified "true believers." In our day certain legalists require the same sort of external conformity.

The problem began to focus for the young pastor. The reason the "sheep" in his church were having trouble identifying the "wolves" in their midst was simple: The church had allowed a superficial outward symbol to become an identifying mark for Christians. And because the intruders had adopted the same mark, they could not be differentiated from the sheep.

True Holiness Begins on the Inside

Paul assures Timothy: "The Lord knows those who are his. . . . Everyone who confesses the name of the Lord must turn away from wickedness" (2 Timothy 2:19). God looks at the inside—at our hearts. And it is from the inside that true fruit appears on the outside, manifesting itself in language and actions that are pleasing to the Lord. These perceptible traits have their roots and origins on the inside. And that makes all the difference between true holiness and false holiness.

A holiness established on the superficial, visible, external aspects of our Christian subculture is in reality a dangerous false holiness. It can lead us to complacency in our walk with the Master. It can lead to a sensory kind of satisfaction that leaves us unsatisfied.

When does holiness begin? To put it simply, it begins when we seek after God. It begins as we yield our entire being to the Lordship of Jesus Christ. It continues as we continue to yield ourselves daily to the indwelling and filling of God's Holy Spirit, as we hunger and thirst after righteousness. It continues as we allow the Spirit to develop and use the spiritual gifts He has given us. Then, and only in those ways, do we begin to minimize the danger of false holiness. Only in that way do we begin to know the power of God's Spirit working within us to produce spiritual fruit in our lives.

Satan cannot counterfeit the fruit of the Spirit—love, joy, peace, patience, kindness, goodness, faithfulness, gentleness and self-control (Galatians 5:22-23). He can produce the spectacular manifestations, he can encourage prescribed dress codes and life-styles, but he cannot produce—nor does he want to produce—an internal life-changing experience brought about only by the power of the indwelling Holy Spirit.

Only by God's Holy Spirit

This fruit of the Spirit is possible only through the presence and controlling activity of the Holy Spirit. That is why Satan and the world he controls want us to judge things on the basis of superficialities. In that way illusion appears to be reality and false holiness can lead to seduction and possible destruction.

So how do we counter false holiness? Let's return to the sheep analogy. We counter false holiness by listening to the voice of the Good Shepherd (John 10:3). We must make sure we are following Him (10:4) and not a thief or a robber—or, worse, a wolf! We need to be aware of our weaknesses, especially our tendency to follow the wrong leader. Quality time with Jesus will help us distinguish His voice from all the other voices seeking our attention.

All of this requires, first, a conscious decision on our part and, second, a commitment to follow through. It is work, and work requires effort. True holiness is never easy. False holiness always is.

My young pastor friend in Gabon discovered that we cannot judge by something as superficial as a head scarf. He learned that his responsibility, as leader of the church, was to develop his flock to know Christ and to grow in Him. As he began to do that, insisting on the role and place of the Holy Spirit in each person's life, the church began to grow, both quantitatively and, more importantly, qualitatively.

Deep down inside, isn't it Jesus whom we really want? For a time we may be infatuated by the externals and follow along with the crowd. But when we take time to stop and listen, God's gentle whisper (see 1 Kings 19:12) calls us back to Jesus. At that point a daily yielding to God's Holy Spirit, a consistent study of the Scriptures, a meaningful prayer life, a witness to others—and everything begins to fall into place normally and naturally.

Why? Because God is making us holy *from the inside.*

We can only become holy through the holiness of God. To try to imitate God will not do; we must receive Him, then reflect His life and nature in our lives. "It is because of Him that you are in Christ Jesus, who has become for us wisdom from God—that is, our righteousness, holiness and redemption" (1 Corinthians 1:30).
—A.B. Simpson—

Holy Fire,
Holy Lives

by Fred A. Hartley, III

I T IS NOT ENOUGH SIMPLY to build an altar. The landscape is cluttered with altars: some Buddhist, some materialistic, some Hebrew, some even Christian.

We evangelicals have built more than our share—private altars, family altars, small group altars, congregational altars, even citywide and worldwide altars. Building altars and bowing at them can be as barren for us as it is for the Buddhists. The question is not, "Do you spend time at an altar?" The question is rather, "Is there holy fire on your altar?"

Elijah, the Hebrew prophet, was on target when he challenged idolatrous Jews to a showdown that would demonstrate once and for all the difference between true holy fire and hollow religious form. He said to the large assembly of people on Mount Carmel, "The god who answers by fire—he is God" (1 Kings 18:24).

A Vision of More

After five years in flat Florida, my wife, two

children and I flew into mountainous Denver, Colorado. I was scheduled to address a bookseller's convention at a resort in Snow Mass, beyond Aspen. It was evening before our flight reached Denver. Most of the trip by rental car to Snow Mass was in darkness and through fog; we did not arrive until after midnight.

The next morning we slept in, then went for a late breakfast. Walking back to our chalet after breakfast, we lifted our heads and could not believe our eyes. There were enormous, majestic, snow-capped mountains! Obviously, they had been there all along, but for the first time we noticed them.

Immediately we got in our car and drove out to get a closer look at the awesome scenery. As I was driving and at the same time looking at the splendor of the mountains, I became aware that a trooper was signaling me over. It happened to be the Fourth of July weekend.

"Are you drunk?" the trooper wanted to know. I assured the officer that although I had certain problems, alcohol was not one of them.

"You see, officer, we're from Florida. We've been so overwhelmed by the imposing Colorado Rockies, I suppose I have not been keeping my eyes on the road as much as I should!" With a smile of understanding, the policeman accepted my explanation and we continued our sightseeing.

When it comes to the Colorado mountains, there is *more*. And when it comes to Christ, there is more—much more. When it comes to the fullness and the holiness of Christ and all there is in Him, we too often are in the darkness and in the fog. Even in times of private or public worship, there is much more in Christ than we normally observe. If only the fog would break up so we could see Christ in all His majesty and splendor! Then we would begin to recognize how much more of Him is yet to be discovered.

Paul not only saw that there was much more in Christ, but he prayed for much more of Christ for the church. We gain a glimpse of his private altar when he says to the Ephesians, "I keep asking that the God of our Lord Jesus Christ, the glorious Father, may give you the Spirit of wisdom and of revelation, so that you may know him better" (Ephesians 1:17).

Paul saw that there was more. He desired more, he asked for more and he received more.

Don't Settle for Less

There are dangers if we fail to see that there is more in Christ. There are pitfalls if we instead choose to settle for less.

1. There is *the danger of apostasy*. Jesus foresaw this and warned His followers: "Watch out that no one deceives you. For many will come in my name, claiming, 'I am the Christ,' and will deceive many. . . . At that time many will turn away from the faith and will betray and hate each other, and many false prophets will appear and deceive many people. Because of the increase of wickedness, the love of most will grow cold" (Matthew 24:4-12).

In our own day, the great antagonists of the gospel are those who have had a previous affiliation with the Christian faith, but since they did not find more in Christ, they went searching for another Christ. Unfortunately, not everyone who starts with God stays with God.

2. There is *the danger of apathy*. One of the commonest sins being confessed in the church today is the sin of apathy. How is it possible to give a half heart to a whole Christ? The answer: We cannot. We give a half heart to a half Christ. Our problem is that when we see only part of Christ we give Him only half a heart. We create our own apathy when we fail to see how much more there is in Christ.

3. There is *the danger of atrophy—paralysis, inertia*. It requires the whole Christ to mobilize the whole church to reach the whole world. We will never reach the whole world with less than a whole Christ. The reason we are partially immobilized is because we are not seeing how much more there is in Christ Jesus.

4. There is *the danger of exhaustion*. If our enemy cannot stop us through inactivity, he will attempt to stop us through overactivity. When the Los Angeles riots broke open in the spring of 1992, *Time* Magazine editor Lance Morrow said, "America is in certain ways a whole country out of control—drugs, crime and more than anything, what has become a borderless wandering." Perhaps we evangelicals have lacked focus and lost navigational skills. We, too, have been guilty of "borderless wandering." Increasingly, when we ask friends, "How are you doing?" they answer, "I am busy—much too busy." We seem to do more and more but accomplish less and less. That is what happens when we lose sight of the much more there is in Christ.

5. There is *the danger of abandonment*. In the 1970s Jacques Ellul described our culture in his book, *Hope in an Age of Abandonment*. His diagnosis: Our culture increasingly has the sense that nothing can be changed, that everything will continue just

as it is and we will be left exclusively to our own devices. Obviously, we can disagree theologically with Ellul's assessment, but in our hearts we might more honestly admit, "Yes, there does seem to be a sense of abandonment." We as believers will feel impotent and abandoned if we lose sight of the fact that in Christ there is always much more.

Ali Hoffad's Diamonds

In contrast to these five dangers, the Holy Spirit wants to renew our vision of the whole Christ. He can instantly roll back the spiritual fog, enabling us once more to experience a dramatic spiritual awakening that will bring tangible changes.

One of the most famous speeches in American history was Russell Conwell's "Acres of Diamonds." Conwell gave it thousands of times throughout the land. He would enter a town or city and interview the mayor, librarians, postmaster, ministers, factory workers. His purpose in the interviews was to discover missed opportunities within the community. Then he would tell the story of Ali Hoffad, and apply it to the local situation.

Ali Hoffad was an Arab who lived between the Tigris and Euphrates Rivers. He owned a large farm with orchards, grain fields and gardens. But Ali Hoffad was enticed by the luster of gold and diamonds. He wanted a piece of the action.

Selling his holdings, Ali set out on his search for diamonds. He traveled through the Middle East, North Africa and Europe. At last he ended up in Barcelona, Spain, an old man clad in rags, trapped in wretchedness and poverty.

The man who bought Ali Hoffad's farm was watering his camel at the garden brook one day when he noticed something sparkling in the stream. It was a black stone, and it reflected all the colors of the rainbow. Fascinated by its beauty, he took it to the house and placed it on the fireplace mantel.

A traveling friend, to whom the householder had offered hospitality, saw the stone and asked where he had found the *diamond!* The two went out to the stream and, to their mutual amazement, found dozens of other diamonds. No matter where they looked, in virtually every square yard of soil, they found diamonds. Ali Hoffad's property became one of the most famous diamond mines in the world, the diamond mine of Golcanda. The largest jewels in the crowns of monarchs in Russia, England and around the world came from Golcanda.

Poor Ali Hoffad! Unwittingly he had sold a diamond mine in order to go off in search of treasure. A lifetime of looking brought him only poverty and ultimately death. But the very land he abandoned contained acres of diamonds.

There is more Ali Hoffad in each of us than we care to admit. We who have salvation in Christ often live lives that are spiritually impoverished and even unholy because we fail to discover the fullness of riches available to us in Him.

A Vision of Receiving

The secret of holiness is not only seeing that there is more in Christ, but receiving more of Christ.

When I heard Armin Gesswein, the great revivalist, say, "There is a difference between praying for revival and revival-praying," my ears perked up.

"When we merely pray for revival," Gesswein continued, "we can pray ourselves into unbelief—praying revival further off into the distance all the time. That is not revival-praying. Revival-praying is when we receive at least a portion of the very thing we are praying toward. Jesus not only wants us to be askers; He wants us to be receivers."

That truth has the potential of revolutionizing not only our prayer lives but also our life-styles.

Think about it: God created us to be receivers. Prior to creating human beings, God was complete in Himself. He did not create us out of a sense of need. He created us out of His fullness in order to have receivers to whom He could benevolently lavish His gifts.

Christian life begins when we receive Christ Jesus, God's Son, into our lives. "He came to that which was his own, but his own did not receive him. Yet to all who received him, to those who believed in his name, he gave the right to become children of God" (John 1:11-12). And as we continue to receive from Jesus, we continue to grow and thrive.

Receiving Is Humbling

The fact is, receiving is humbling. It is an admission that apart from Christ we can do nothing of eternal worth. We have nothing to give except that which He has first given us. When we recognize that great truth, we are in a position to serve the Lord.

Receiving is sanctifying. In receiving God's good gifts, it must not be for the sake of receiving from God. We seek and we receive in order to *give*. If our motive in seeking God is simply to receive His gifts, we begin our quest selfishly. First we must let God cleanse us from selfishness. We will not receive from God until our selfishness is cleansed.

Seeking in order to receive and give convinces us that God is the source of all good things. The Lord Jesus wants us to feed out of His hand. Do we not pray, "Give us today our daily bread" (Matthew 6:11)? Actually, every facet of the Lord's Prayer involves receiving in one way or another. God wants us to learn how to pray with cupped hands.

A Vision of Fresh Fire

And what, precisely is it that we are to be receiving from God?

Primarily, Christ intends for us to receive a fresh revelation of who He is so that we can know Him better and bring Him greater glory in our service.

One present-day tragedy: We have grown accustomed to altars without fire. How is it that with all the altars in the land, with all the quiet times and Christian churches and Christian bookstores and Christian colleges and Christian seminaries and Christian radio and television and Christian organizations—with all these altars in the land—immorality is spreading like an epidemic? Can it be that we have not had God's holy fire upon our altars? Worse, could it be that we think altars without fire are *normal*?

Elijah, who knew how to pray down both fire and rain from heaven, said, "The god who answers by fire—he is God."

Perhaps today, more than 2,800 years later, God is awaking His church to the fact that we must not feel smug because we are pausing for a daily quiet time at our private altar, or because we are leading our children in a family altar, or because we attend a midweek prayer altar. It is not enough to have form without fire.

God desires to send the fire of His holiness to our altars. Without it, our piety is little more than a religious shell, and we risk losing our children to other gods. Whether at our own private altar or family altar or church altar, we must boldly declare that the God who answers by fire is God. We need His holy fire. We need holy lives.

Are We Praying for God's Fire?

We can join Charles Haddon Spurgeon who prayed this prayer 150 years ago:

> *Father, send us the Holy Spirit. Send us the wind of spiritual life and the fire of unconquerable zeal.*
>
> *You are our God. Answer us, O God, by fire. Send us the wind and the fire, and then we shall see You to be God indeed.*
>
> *The kingdom comes not, and the work is flagging. O that You would send the wind and the fire! And you will do this when we are all in one accord, all believing, all expecting, all prepared by prayer.*

One of a firefighter's nightmares is known as "backdraft." Fire needs three elements: fuel, heat and oxygen. Backdraft occurs when oxygen is introduced into an environment where fuel (combustible material) and heat already exist. In order to avoid this violent explosion, firefighters poke holes in the roof of burning buildings to allow heat to escape from not-yet-burning sections. Then when oxygen hits, there will not be devastation.

God is preparing to give to His church the greatest revival in world history. He is gathering fuel. He is increasing the heat through fervent prayer. He is prepared to breathe a fresh breath of heaven upon us that will bring about a dynamic moment nothing short of backdraft.

We want to do more than simply talk about holy fire. We want to receive it.

Perhaps our response to such a challenge is to throw up our hands and say in exasperation, "But I'm no Elijah!" In describing Elijah, the first thing James mentions is, "Elijah was a man just like us" (James 5:17). Elijah was a flesh-and-blood human being just like each of us is. He was a seeker who became a receiver of heavenly fire. And God has heavenly fire for all of our altars.

In these days Christ is holding out to His church a vision of *more*. A vision of heavenly, holy fire to burn upon our altars, to purify our hearts and lives, to charge the engines of our service for Christ. Go ahead, pray with cupped hands. Always pray to receive. Enter into God's presence to receive holy fire for holy living.

There is no need to settle for less when Christ offers so much more.

205

CHATER 20	# Holiness, Revival and Prayer

by Armin Gesswein

W E WILL GIVE OURSELVES CONTIN-UALLY to prayer and to the ministry of the word" (Acts 6:4 NKJV). In those few well-chosen words the apostles, addressing the Jerusalem church, focused on the *right combination for revival* (prayer and preaching) and the *right order for revival* (prayer, then preaching). Implied also in their statement is the *right place for revival* (the local church).

In the original Greek, *prayer* and *the ministry of the word* are combined and dominated by a single, strong verb meaning to persevere in, to be steadfast in. After a considerable time period and amazing church growth, these apostles were still keeping right on with the same "Upper Room" praying that preceded Pentecost and the same intensive ministry of the Word that had added so remarkably to the church.

That's exactly the way it is with fire. It exists by burning, and the fuel, the oxygen and the heat that got it started are what keep it burning—if they continue to be in the right combination. Many who are

206

now praying for revival are unclear on these very things.

Revival Praying, Revival Preaching

Today there is plenty of praying for revival that brings no revival. For one thing, how did we get into this terrible *rut of passivity*? Especially when God all the while is actively calling us—even blasting His trumpet to get us into it—to repent and get on fire for God *now*.

It seems we would rather pray on and on for some big revival "out there" than to pray for a big revival "in here" in our own lives. Our praying for revival amounts to nothing—nothing happens—until and unless we pray, "Let it begin in *me*."

The leaders of the Jerusalem congregation also clarify for us the second great ingredient for revival: the ministry of the Word. Jesus commanded that "repentance and forgiveness of sins . . . be preached in his name to all nations, beginning at Jerusalem" (Luke 24:47). Not just forgiveness, but *repentance* and forgiveness. Today forgiveness is being preached right and left, but without repentance. And there is no change, no holiness, no revival.

Repentance must be preached. It must be preached in the spirit of prayer, or it does not take hold. So often we have to learn that lesson the hard way. Our preaching backfires or misfires or there is no fire!

I Prepare to Preach the Word

God called me to be a minister of the Word, a preacher. All our family were Lutherans. You could shake any branch of our family tree and you would shake only Lutherans. Moreover, we were a particular brand of Lutherans—very strict. We did not even mix with other Lutherans! (Thankfully, that has changed.)

But one thing we continually stressed: We wanted to be people of the Word. When we said *Sola Scriptura* (Scripture only), we meant it.

In 1931 I graduated from Concordia Theological Seminary in St. Louis and received the call to be "missionary-at-large." That meant I was to start—plant—new Lutheran churches.

On August 2 I was ordained along with two other graduates in St. John's Lutheran Church, LaPorte, Indiana. The large sanctuary was very full. A fine preacher, one of the vice-presidents of the synod, preached on the text, "The harvest truly is plenteous, but the labourers are few; pray ye therefore the Lord of the harvest that he will send forth labourers into his harvest" (Matthew 9:37-38 KJV).

In one of his climaxes the preacher almost thundered down at the three of us who were seated on chairs in the front: "Young men, LABORERS! Not 8 hours, not 10 hours, not 12 hours—often NIGHT AND DAY!" I'll never forget it.

The next morning some relatives and friends saw me off on the train for Long Island and the community where, by God's grace, I would start a church.

A Life-Changing Discovery

It was a tough town of about 3,000 people. Sin was strong and vice somewhat rooted. I soon found out that no preaching had disturbed it. I went right to work. I rented a school auditorium for our Sunday services. I had been taught to push doorbells, and I did a lot of that. I soon got to know the town and became very burdened for it in prayer.

Soon people were coming to church. After three months we organized with a board of 12 men. (Jesus had 12 disciples, and I thought we should have a board of 12.)

Then I made a discovery—one that completely changed my life, my ministry and my understanding of the church. I had begun to read the Acts. The first thing I saw was that Jesus also was starting a church—*His* first church—and His way was very different from the way I was going about it. I read: "Then [the disciples] returned to Jerusalem. . . . When they arrived, they went upstairs to the room where they were staying. . . . They all joined together constantly in prayer, along with the women and Mary the mother of Jesus, and with his brothers" (Acts 1:12-14).

"That's a prayer meeting!" I exclaimed to myself. We did not have such prayer meetings in our 2-million-member denomination. I had never been in a prayer meeting, but somehow I had built up a very negative mental image of one—a fanatical, wild sort of thing, not conducted "decently and in order."

But an earlier verse in the chapter shattered my misconception with one swift blow. *Jesus* called them to that prayer meeting. "Do not leave Jerusalem," He said, "but wait for the gift my Father promised" (Acts 1:4). The Jesus I loved, the Jesus who called me to start this church—*He* called that Jerusalem prayer meeting! It shut my mouth at once for any arguments against prayer meetings. It tenderized me. It also toughened me. I knew instinctively that if I went through with this discovery, I would have to be tough as well as tender.

I Announce a Prayer Meeting

Very soon, one Sunday morning, I announced a prayer meeting and invited my congregation to come. That simple announcement, in a tone of voice not too animated, must have had a lot of power per word. It began to echo and reecho among the members. "A prayer meeting? What's that?" "A prayer meeting? Did we hear correctly?" "What's happening to our young minister?" "This is going to ruin our church!"

I had announced the prayer meeting for Saturday evening, to be held in a large home that a man and his wife had opened to us. Talk about a long week! Friday night I could hardly sleep. *Who will be there—especially the way people are talking? I know I'll be there if the Lord spares me. And I know that man and his wife will be there, because they can't very well get out of it. I wonder who else will come.*

Saturday evening finally arrived. I wanted to be the first one there. I was! Waiting in the kitchen were the man and his wife, nicely dressed. Next to the kitchen was the large room all lit up and ready for the crowd. We were nervous and said little. The clock struck eight—the appointed hour. So the three of us went into the room and sat down. Just then one of our deacons came in. By his own later admission he was not yet a Christian, but he thought he ought to be loyal to me. So he came.

Each of us had a Bible. I began: "I really don't know much more than you do about a prayer meeting, but this is what I found in God's Word." And then we read Acts 1:14. All three of them agreed,

"That's a prayer meeting. It's clear." Even the un-converted deacon saw it. (I should add that he was soon converted and never missed our prayer meetings.)

We then took plenty of time to read from other places in the Acts. We read from Acts 4 about that mighty prayer meeting where God shook the place and answered with powerful new wonders in and through the church. We read from Acts 12 about the all-night prayer meeting that saw Peter delivered from prison with many more new and powerful developments as a result.

No Sermon Needed

The four of us in one corner of that big room never needed a sermon on the prayer meeting. Just through the reading of the plain Word of God we became prayer meeting Christians.

Soon the four of us went to our knees. Each of us prayed. Simply. Earnestly. Briefly. Even the unconverted deacon prayed. It was one of the shortest prayer sessions I have ever attended! In a few minutes we were all up from our knees. Charles Spurgeon once remarked, "It's not always the length, it's the depth that counts!"

Jesus began to bless our church and its ministry in new ways. Soon we needed that large room for our prayer meetings. I began to teach my people to pray, and we learned together. In answer to the praying at those prayer meetings, many good things began to happen. For one, I began to learn to fellowship with Christians of other denominations and backgrounds. They, too, began to come to our prayer meetings.

It wasn't long before my preaching also began to change. Praying put new muscle into my messages and ministry. In turn the preaching, backed by the praying, moved us into one of the strongest revivals I have ever been in—and I have been in many, including the great Norway revival. It was not as widespread a revival as many, but it was as deep. It went right to the taproot of conscience. There was conviction of sin and sincere repentance, there was God's gracious forgiveness and there were strong conversions. People touched God's holiness and their lives were radically changed.

What the Word Said to Me

The revival broke out one Sunday morning at what was supposed to be our Communion service. As I got around in the town, I began to hear reports of wild Saturday night parties (the very night of our prayer meetings). And some of my leading members were participants.

I heard other disturbing things involving some of our church members. It was one of those towns where everybody knows everybody else. These reports made my heart heavy, but I didn't know what to do about it all. What brought it to a head was the upcoming Communion service. These people would be taking Communion again, but they would go on living the same old way.

Shall I ever forget that Sunday? The day before, on Saturday, I had fasted and prayed. I didn't know anything about fasting, but the burden on my heart was so heavy that I didn't want to eat. I spent the day before the Lord, much of it on my knees with my Bible. I sought and besought the Lord in prayer:

"What can I do, what should I do, what must I do tomorrow at the Communion? It is to be a *holy* Communion, and some of my members are living in unholy communion—in sin, even in drunkenness. They are a stumbling block to the people of this town."

Using the Bible as my prayer book, I kept going through its pages. In First Corinthians I read:

> Do you not know that the wicked will not inherit the kingdom of God? Do not be deceived: Neither the sexually immoral nor idolaters nor adulterers nor male prostitutes nor homosexual offenders nor thieves nor the greedy nor drunkards nor slanderers nor swindlers will inherit the kingdom of God. And that is what some of you were. But you were washed, you were sanctified, you were justified in the name of the Lord Jesus Christ and by the Spirit of our God. (1 Corinthians 6:9-11)

I was heartened by the past tense: "That is what some of you *were*." In other words, not any longer. They were washed, sanctified, justified. How wonderful! That is what revival did in the Corinthian congregation. They had got rid of the "old yeast" so they could "keep the Festival" (1 Corinthians 5:7-8).

In Galatians my eyes fell on some Scripture I had not seen before—Scripture that exactly hit and fit my situation.

> The acts of the sinful nature are obvious: sexual immorality, impurity and debauchery; idolatry and witchcraft; hatred, discord, jealousy, fits of

213

*rage, selfish ambition, dissensions, factions and
envy; drunkenness, orgies, and the like. I warn
you, as I did before, that those who live like this
will not inherit the kingdom of God.* (Galatians
5:19-21)

I wrote these and other Scriptures down in my
notebook. I felt armed with the sword of the Spirit,
the Word of God. I was charged—and ready to
charge. I was ready to preach "repentance and forgiveness of sins" in my "Jerusalem."

Communion Sunday Revival

Sunday came—our Communion Sunday. I was
ready. The weather was beautiful. I was carrying a
new gown which our Ladies' Society had just given
me for my birthday. I was to wear it for the first
time—for the Communion Sunday service. But as I
entered the school house I felt as if I was clothed in
another way, with the presence and power of the
Holy Spirit. Inside the building I met a man, and
then another—both fighting back the tears. I didn't
know much then about the Holy Spirit, but I sensed
His "holy hush" over the audience. As I went to the
pulpit I took with me my Bible and the notebook
into which the day before I had written those Scriptures and some application.

"This is Communion Sunday," I began, "but I'm
going to withhold Communion today because I
know there are those here who are not ready for
Communion. I also know there are those here who
are ready, but I believe they will gladly forbear because there are some who are not."

Lutherans have a very high view of the Sacrament;

I knew it was serious for a young minister just out of seminary to withhold Communion. But to me, that was just the point: I was upholding the sacredness of the Communion by not letting it be desecrated by those who were living in unholy communion with "the devil, the world and the flesh," which all had promised to "renounce."

As I began to preach what the Lord had laid on my heart, the Holy Spirit began to take my thoughts. I sensed His holy power and an uncharacteristic boldness. The Word became a sword cutting through any kind of opposition.

The Holy Spirit broke through, bringing conviction of guilt, righteousness and judgment (see John 16:8).

I had had no experience "giving invitations" or making "altar calls." But as I concluded, I said, "Those who mean to repent of their sins today, please kneel where you are. But don't kneel because you see someone else kneeling. Don't kneel unless you mean it. I'll kneel here at the Communion altar and ask the Lord to have mercy on us, forgive our sins and remove the blot on our ministry in this town."

I did this with fear and trembling. To my surprise, at least half the audience knelt, some in the aisle, some weeping, repenting of their sins. Some, during my preaching, had already repented and turned to Christ.

Life-Changing Consequences

That day remarkable conversions took place. It required the strong power of the Spirit in a revival to reach those people. All the converts became prayer meeting Christians. Some would walk several miles to get to a prayer meeting. A few were ready to pray half nights. They loved prayer and prayer meetings. Prayer became primary. And God answered prayer for them in many ways, not only solving their problems but changing their lives and changing people through them.

What about holiness? We didn't know much about holiness as a special teaching. But we certainly experienced the holiness of God and of His Holy Spirit. We knew what sin was in the presence of a holy God. We knew that to be saved meant to be saved from our sins. We were no longer to continue in sin.

I walked out of the school building that day sensing the Holy Spirit at work in the very atmosphere of the town. And it was so. People began to be reached and won to Christ who would never listen before. The Communion elements were still on the altar, untouched. Revival had come instead, bringing us to repentance and the forgiveness of sins. Jesus had ministered His divine life to us, fitting us for holy Communion by giving us communion with Himself.

God changed me. As I left the service that morning, the Holy Spirit suddenly, clearly, definitely called me to a revival ministry. In the depths of my being He was saying, "Revival is your ministry."

I knew it then. And the call is just as clear to me today as it was that day.

Holiness in the Church

by D. Paul McGarvey

NOT TOO LONG AGO, MY family and I accompanied my mother's "earthly tent" to its place of rest in a small rural church cemetery amid the gently rolling hills of central Pennsylvania.

By the testimony of all who knew her, she lived a consistent life of faith in and obedience to Jesus Christ, her Lord and Savior. My mother was a holy woman who lived a holy life.

Many of the people buried in that small cemetery are my relatives. The nearby church was their place of Christian nurture—some for a lifetime, others, like my parents, until they themselves became nurturers in full-time Christian service. They were holy people who lived obedient, godly lives.

As I walked among the headstones with the familiar names, I began to ask myself if my generation would be known as holy to those who lay us to rest. I am haunted by the question. Its answer is elusive. What made my mother and those among whom she is buried holy? What exactly *is* holiness? How did the people of that little church come to

live in such a way that I and others call them holy?
What makes anything holy?

Holiness Defined

God alone is holy in essence. "Who is like you—
majestic in holiness?" sang Moses and the Israelites
(Exodus 15:11) after God delivered them at the Red
Sea. God Himself declared His holiness to Israel
(Leviticus 11:44-45; 19:2; 21:8). Isaiah heard the
heavenly seraphs calling to one another, "Holy,
holy, holy is the LORD Almighty" (Isaiah 6:3). Mary,
Jesus' mother, said, "The Mighty One has done
great things for me— / holy is his name" (Luke
1:49).

In his vision of heaven, the apostle John heard the
four living creatures around the throne unendingly
declare, "Holy, holy, holy is the Lord God Almighty" (Revelation 4:8). Later he heard the
heavenly victors in a similar refrain: "O Lord, . . .
you alone are holy" (Revelation 15:4).

God is holy. It is His essence. The Scriptures use
the word *holy* to describe people, angels, ground,
Mount Sinai, altars, offerings, vessels, Jerusalem and
other cities, the temple, the nation Israel, the Scriptures themselves, the New Jerusalem. These God
made holy—and is making holy—cleansing, purify-
ing, consecrating, setting apart for His purposes.
God's very presence sets them apart from the ordinary and the natural for His extraordinary and supernatural purposes.

A holy person is one cleansed of ungodliness, set
apart to do God's will. He or she stands in God's
stead without claim upon life or possession, a
habitation of the Holy One.

The Need for Holiness in the Church

Mother's graduation to heaven has made a difference on earth. She faithfully prayed for me. I felt her prayers. I miss them. She prayed for missionaries. They are weakened because she is no longer "holding up their arms."

Mother encouraged disheartened friends by her telephone calls. She has no telephone in heaven. Younger women who looked to her as an example have only her memory now. While she lived on earth she made a remarkable difference in many lives. The same can be said of most of the others in that little cemetery. They made an eternal difference in many lives.

Does today's church have what it takes to impact this generation? Do I?

Holiness is needed in the church because *people are alienated from God.* God desires to reconcile such people to Himself and welcome them to His heaven, free from evil associations and holy (see Colossians 1:21-22). God's holy commandments have proven to people that they are lawbreakers by nature and under condemnation of death as unholy (Romans 7:7-13; 1 Timothy 1:8-11).

A day of reckoning is coming, marked by the destruction of the heavens and the earth and the judgment and destruction of ungodly people (2 Peter 3:1-12). Without holiness in the church, to which God has given the ministry and the message of reconciliation (2 Corinthians 5:17-21), what hope is there for unholy people? Without a church that is the "aroma of Christ" among those who are perishing (2 Corinthians 2:15), what prospect of salvation remains for the sinner?

Holiness in the church is needed *to make an eternal difference in the lives of those who are without hope!* If the church is unholy and preoccupied with its own concerns, where shall the hopeless turn? By pointing people to Jesus Christ, who is "able to save completely those who come to God through him" (Hebrews 7:25), a holy church closes the gap between a holy God and unholy people.

The Church Is God's Temple

Holiness is needed in the church because *the church is the "temple" of God, the Holy Spirit.* In his correspondence with the Corinthian church, Paul addresses the problem of factions within the church. He reminds his readers:

> *Don't you know that you yourselves [plural] are God's temple [singular] and that God's Spirit lives in you [plural]? If anyone destroys God's temple [singular], God will destroy him; for God's temple is sacred [holy], and you [plural] are that temple [singular].* (1 Corinthians 3:16-17)

In a unique way God has chosen to indwell the collective body of Christ by His Spirit. Those guilty of fracturing this unity must be either unaware of God's will and purpose or disdainful of it. Whichever, the resulting "destruction" keeps this holy temple from being the witness God desires it to be to His reconciling power.

This disunity is epidemic in our day. At every turn willful people within the church (even pastors at times!) seem to have no reticence to threaten the unity of the church body by gossip, power-brokering, fault-finding, complaining and pouting. There is an emergency-level need to harness these divisive attitudes and this diabolical behavior! Holy living must mark every member of the body. Nothing less will let the church be a center of spiritual power to overcome evil!

If God's Spirit inhabits the church as a whole, so does He indwell its individual members. It is inconceivable that the Spirit who indwells believers could condone the mistreatment of one believer by another. We must have holiness in the church to cancel the incredible malice too often evident among so-called believers. Otherwise, what difference can the church be expected to make in its world?

The Call to Holiness in the Church

Some think holiness is not expected of all Christians. They suppose it is for those who are *really serious* about their faith. They may excuse their own failure by protesting that they are "only human."

No Christian is perfect in thought, word or deed. Each remains in need of God's grace and continued pardon. But too many Christians are satisfied to walk a low spiritual path. The *normal* biblical expectation of "leaving everything to follow Jesus" (Luke 5:11) is far from where they live. Listen to the New Testament call to holiness:

> *Therefore, I urge you, brothers, in view of God's mercy, to offer your bodies as living sacrifices, holy and pleasing to God—this is your spiritual act of worship.* (Romans 12:1)

Let us purify ourselves from everything that contaminates body and spirit, perfecting holiness out of reverence to God. (2 Corinthians 7:1)

Put on the new self, created to be like God in true righteousness and holiness. (Ephesians 4:24)

It is God's will that you should be sanctified. . . . God did not call us to be impure, but to live a holy life. (1 Thessalonians 4:3, 7)

God . . . has saved us and called us to a holy life. (2 Timothy 1:8-9)

Make every effort to live in peace with all men and to be holy; without holiness no one will see the Lord. (Hebrews 12:14)

Just as he who called you is holy, so be holy in all you do; for it is written: "Be holy, because I am holy." (1 Peter 1:15).

Impossible as it seems, holy should be the normal Christian way of life. Holiness is not for a select few! God calls all of us to holiness.

The Evidence of Holiness in the Church

What does a holy church look like? How will we know when a local church is walking in holiness and when it is not? The Word of God is our final authority for faith and conduct. In it there are specific descriptions of holiness that can enable us to evaluate a church's level of holiness.

Separation. In the Old Testament era, Israel was to

be a nation separate from the surrounding nations. The New Testament people of God—the church—have also been called to separate themselves from all that is unholy. Paul applies God's Old Testament call to Israel to be a separated people to the New Testament church. He says, "Let us purify ourselves from everything that contaminates body and spirit, perfecting holiness out of reverence for God" (2 Corinthians 7:1).

Intimacy. Heathen nations hoped to keep their deities at a safe distance. They designed and carried out their sacrifices with that in mind. But when the Lord God instituted the Old Testament sacrificial system, He did so to bring Him and His people closer together. Like with Israel, God desires a close relationship with His New Testament church.

God loved us so much that He gave His Son, Jesus Christ, to be the final, complete and perfect sacrifice to reconcile us to Himself. It was a love and it was a provision that extends to the whole world (John 3:16). How can our response be other than love?

Obedience. If we love God, we will obey Him (John 14:21). We must beware a false security that causes us to devalue our unique personal relationship with God. We must guard against treating carelessly God's Word designed to set us apart for His holy purposes.

Romans 12 is a smorgasbord of guidelines for holy living. All of them are predicated on the "living sacrifice" of ourselves to God (12:1). *Living sacrifices must make a conscious effort to stay on the altar.*

As the chapter goes on to say, our humble, generous, diligent, cheerful exercise of our appointed ministries within the church, for the good of all, evidences our holiness. Obedience to God's word is nonnegotiable!

Conclusion

What will be the impact of holiness in the church of Jesus Christ? Paul makes a significant comment to the church in Rome:

> *Now that you have been set free from sin and have become slaves to God, the benefit you reap leads to holiness, and the result is eternal life. For the wages of sin is death, but the gift of God is eternal life in Christ Jesus our Lord.* (Romans 6:22-23)

I match those words with Peter's, written likewise to believers, though Jewish by background:

> *You are a chosen people, a royal priesthood, a holy nation, a people belonging to God, that you may declare the praises of him who called you out of darkness into his wonderful light.* (1 Peter 2:9)

Holy is what the church is supposed to be. God intends its members to think and act like holy people. God the Holy Spirit indwells each genuine believer. He inhabits the church to empower it to think and act in holiness. God's holy Word is its guidebook.

One other thing is necessary and often lacking: *Obedience.* Arraigned before the Jewish Sanhedrin, Peter and the other apostles declared they "must obey God rather than men!" (Acts 5:29). They went on to say:

The God of our fathers raised Jesus from the dead—whom you had killed by hanging him on a tree. God exalted him to his own right hand as Prince and Savior that he might give repentance and forgiveness of sins to Israel. We are witnesses of these things, and so is the Holy Spirit, whom God has given to those who obey him. (Acts 5:30-32)

God gives the Holy Spirit to those who obey Him. God makes holy those who conform to His precepts detailed in the Bible. Only if our generation learns to *obey God* will our children and grandchildren who one day lay our earthly remains to rest say of us, "They were holy people."

God is our standard, and as His children we must be like Him. No lower standard will pass. We must not aim to be as good as some people; we must not excuse ourselves because we are no worse than others. It is God who is our pattern. "Be perfect, therefore, as your heavenly Father is perfect" (Matthew 5:48).
—A.B. Simpson—

<table>
<tr><td>CHAPTER</td></tr>
<tr><td>22</td></tr>
</table>

	Holiness and
CHAPTER	the Spiritual
22	Gifts

Holiness and the Spiritual Gifts

CHAPTER

22

by John E. Packo

FOR A GROWING NUMBER OF churches today, spiritual gifts are the "in thing." The charismatic movement of the late 1950s and early 1960s is largely responsible. Church growth advocates have done their part, demonstrating the value of spiritual gifts to effective ministry and numerical growth.

As in the church at Corinth, there is no lack of gifts in use today. As in the church at Corinth, there are the same excesses and abuses.

In Corinth, the missing ingredient was holiness. There was a lack of holy living. Is this not also the missing ingredient in today's church world? *A lifestyle of holiness is essential if our spiritual gifts are to glorify God.* If we are going to return the credibility and relevance of the church to our culture, we need to reexamine the gifts in the light of biblical holiness.

Positional Holiness Won't Do

In the opening lines of his first letter to the

church at Corinth, Paul establishes the relationship between holiness and the spiritual gifts. He addresses the church as *positionally* holy: ". . . sanctified in Christ Jesus and called to be holy" (1 Corinthians 1:2). He acknowledges their possession of the spiritual gifts: "You do not lack any spiritual gift" (1:7). But he concludes that they are worldly and behaving as unsaved people: "You are still worldly. . . . Are you not acting like mere men?"

Their problem was the lack of *experiential* holiness. They did not lack any spiritual gift, but they lacked a life-style of holiness. Spiritual gifts without experiential holiness abuse God's glory, compromise His power and bring the church down to the level of a social club.

The Corinthians had spiritual gifts, but they were not spiritual. Paul calls them "worldly."

Spiritual gifts are not a barometer of holiness. There are at least two reasons for this. First, spiritual gifts are given to *every* believer by the sovereign will of God. The Spirit "gives them to each one, just as he determines" (1 Corinthians 12:11). Their distribution is one of the ministries of the Holy Spirit. It is not the decision of the individual believer. And second, they are given by the grace of God. God's grace inclines Him to bestow benefits upon the undeserving. One of these benefits is spiritual gifts. In fact, the Greek word for *gifts—charismata—*comes from the Greek word for *grace—charis*.

Paul wrote to the Ephesians: "To each one of us grace has been given as Christ apportioned it" (Ephesians 4:7). In Greek it reads "*the* grace has been given . . ." The thought is of the one grace of God distributing a rainbow of gifts.

"By Their Fruit You Will Recognize Them"

Since the gifts of the Spirit are the evidence of neither holiness nor spirituality, what *is* the evidence? And how do the gifts and holiness relate to each other?

The Corinthian believers were not lacking any spiritual gift. But another commodity made possible only through the same Holy Spirit was sadly lacking. The Corinthians lacked the *fruit* of the Spirit.

Jesus approved a reliable test for holiness: "By their fruit you will recognize them" (Matthew 7:16). The presence of *fruit,* not the presence of gifts, is the test of holiness. Satan can counterfeit the spiritual gifts. He would have great difficulty trying to imitate the fruit of the Spirit.

There are three main distinctions between the fruit of the Spirit and the gifts of the Spirit:

- The fruit is what the believer is; the gifts are what he or she does
- The fruit is related to character; the gifts are related to service
- All of the fruit—love, joy, peace, patience, kindness, goodness, faithfulness, gentleness and self-control (Galatians 5:22-23)—should be evident in every mature believer; only certain gifts will be possessed by any one believer

First Corinthians 13, the great love chapter of the Bible, makes it clear that the gifts of the Spirit can never operate in the will of God apart from the fruit of the Spirit.

An Nth Degree Scenario

Paul begins the passage which is First Corinthians 13 in our Bibles with two extreme scenarios:

> *If I speak in the tongues of men and of angels, but have not love, I am only a resounding gong or a clanging cymbal. If I have the gift of prophecy and can fathom all mysteries and all knowledge, and if I have a faith that can move mountains, but have not love, I am nothing.* (13:1-2)

Paul talks of fathoming *all* mysteries, *all* knowledge. He talks of mountain-moving faith. He names two of the most spectacular forms of self-sacrifice known to humanity: giving *all* he possesses to the poor, surrendering *his body to the flames*.

What are these two graphic verses saying to us? When the gifts operate without the fruit—love—they operate in the energy of our flesh. They are unavailing. They are meaningless. That is why Paul called the Corinthians believers "worldly" (3:1).

Despite all their gifts, they defiled their bodies, they were puffed up with pride, they tolerated immorality. They were suing one another in court, they were confused about marriage, they had abused the doctrine of Christian liberty. They had made a mockery of the Lord's Supper, they had corrupted the gifts of the Spirit, they were in ignorance concerning the resurrection. They had even let down in their offerings to the Lord.

The "fruit inspector's" test of ministry is very crucial: *"Is love the motive behind the use of your spiritual gifts?"*

How Do We Get from Here to There?

How can the believer move from a carnal life-style of ministry into a love-motivated life-style of ministry? There is a normal tendency in our fleshly nature to be proud when we are using our spiritual gifts. But whenever the focus is on us or the gift rather than on Jesus Christ, we misuse the gift.

The Corinthian believers had lost sight of the cross and of the Christ of the cross. That is exactly where Paul begins:

> The message of the cross is foolishness to those who are perishing, but to us who are being saved it is the power of God. (1 Corinthians 1:18)

The wise of the world believe the way of the cross is foolishness. Paul reprimands the Corinthians for standing on the wisdom of the world in opposition to the eternal spiritual values of the Christian life. He focuses on the Christ of the cross, declaring their positional standing as believers.

> It is because of [God] that you are in Christ Jesus, who has become for us wisdom from God— that is, our righteousness, holiness and redemption. (1:30)

That is a key verse if we are to put holiness and the spiritual gifts in perspective with Jesus Christ. Paul is saying in effect: "You are now to practice in experience what you have in position. You are to experience Christ's righteousness, holiness and redemption in daily living."

It sounds lofty enough. But how, Paul, do you accomplish that?

Read on.

> When I came to you, brothers, I did not come with eloquence or superior wisdom as I proclaimed to you the testimony about God. For I resolved to know nothing while I was with you except Jesus Christ and him crucified. (2:1-2)

First, he was saying, stop boasting of your achievements like the world does. Self-promotion is not a trait of holiness. Begin boasting in the Lord. Second, remember, you're dead. You were crucified with Christ. When He died, you died. It's the only message you need. Because Paul's life and ministry rested on the crucified life of Christ, it rested not "on men's wisdom, but on God's power" (2:5).

It is the message he wrote to the Galatians. I like the way E.H. Peterson turns Galatians 2:20 in *The Message: The New Testament in Contemporary Language*: "My ego is no longer central. . . . Christ lives in me. The life you see me living is not 'mine,' but it is lived by faith in the Son of God, who loved me and gave himself for me."

The cross was in Paul's thinking when he exhorted the believers in Rome "to offer your bodies as living sacrifices, holy and pleasing to God. . . . Be transformed by the renewing of your mind. Then you will be able to test and approve what God's will is—his good, pleasing and perfect will" (Romans 12:1-2).

Many readers stop with verse two and never realize that 12:3-6 lead into a list of spiritual gifts. We can only conclude that Paul is consistent in this issue of the spirit of the cross and holiness in preparation for ministry of the spiritual gifts.

A poem by Breston T. Badley suggests the relationship when he says to the Savior, "My Jesus, show me thy feet." And then he asks, "Oh God, dare I show thee / My hands and my feet?"

The Church Is Christ's Body

The New Testament uses the human body to illustrate how spiritual relationships should exist in the church, Christ's "body." The three main listings of spiritual gifts (Romans 12, First Corinthians 12, Ephesians 4) are each presented in the context of the body of Christ.

The Holy Spirit of God not only indwells us as individuals but the corporate community of believers, the church, the Body of Christ. Just as we, individually, are indwelt by the Spirit of God, so the entire church is a dwelling place for the Spirit of Christ (see Ephesians 2:22). Jesus remains in the world after His ascension by reproducing in us individually and in the church corporately His life and character. We are to show Christ to the world. Christ is the head of His body, the church.

The term *body* indicates that the church is more than an organization of parts. It is an organism. It shares life between interrelated parts. The sharing of spiritual life and the ministry of the spiritual gifts for the common good of the whole body is the very nature of body life. The gifts are not for private use but for the benefit of the whole body: "To each one the manifestation of the Spirit is given for the common good" (1 Corinthians 12:7).

Paul's analogy of the body in First Corinthians

12:12-27, sandwiched between two lists of spiritual gifts, forms the most detailed account we have of the church as a living organism. Five spiritual relationships are illustrated by the body:

1. We are placed into the body by Spirit-baptism (12:13). Spirit-baptism occurs at the new birth, uniting the new believer with spiritual life and with other believers, engifting him or her for spiritual ministry.

2. The body consists of many parts (12:14).

3. God has arranged the parts of the body as He wants them (12:18).

4. All the parts are needed (12:21-24).

5. The parts have equal concern for each other (12:25-26).

Your Pastor a Gift?

Have you ever thought of your pastor as a gift given by God to you? Although spiritual gifts are not a measure of holiness, the Lord in His plan for the church has given leadership gifts for one ultimate purpose. He wants the church to be Himself in the world, expressing Christ-likeness in its life and ministry. How is this accomplished?

First, God has given spiritual gifts of "apostles, . . . prophets, . . . evangelists, . . . pastors and teachers, to prepare God's people for works of service" (Ephesians 4:11-12). They have a *perfecting* responsibility to the church. The same Greek word is translated *mending* in Matthew 4:21 as Peter, James and John prepared their nets for fish.

Second, the saints who are being "mended" for action have two main responsibilities: (1) the *work of ministry*, using their spiritual gifts, and (2) the *up-*

building of the body of Christ. Building up one another is essential to a healthy body.

Your pastor and other church leaders, with their equipped congregation, are (or should be) striving for three goals:

First, unity of the faith (4:13). When new Christians grow under spiritually gifted teachers, they become sound in doctrine and mature. They are able to stand against any wind of error that would lead them astray (4:14).

Second, knowledge of Christ (4:13). The word *knowledge* is more than head knowledge. It means to know Christ more and more through a growing relationship with Him.

Third, maturity (4:13). Maturity is defined here as "attaining to the whole measure of the fullness of Christ." The church is to become Christ-like.

Four Areas in Which We Are to Mature

This maturing is to take place in four areas, Paul tells the Ephesian Christians.

1. We are to mature in the area of communication. We are to "speak the truth in love" (4:15). The mature believer speaks the truth, period. The mature believer speaks the truth in love.

2. We are to mature in the area of recognizing Christ's authority. We will "in all things grow up into him who is the Head, that is, Christ" (4:15). Our responsibility is to submit to the Lordship of Christ in all things.

3. We are to mature in the area of submission to Christ (4:16). The church grows (a) when each member harmoniously functions in his or her proper place, (b) when some parts supply nourish-

ment and (c) when each member works effectively for the benefit of the whole.

4. We are to mature in the area of building up one another in love (4:16). We go to church to be built up. If divine love is not present, no upbuilding will take place.

Conclusion

Each of us has an obligation to use whatever gift we have received "to serve others, faithfully administering God's grace in its various forms" (1 Peter 4:10). Peter goes on to say: "If anyone serves, he should do it with the strength God provides, so that in all things God may be praised through Jesus Christ"(4:11).

When I was nine, I saw for the first time a glass prism. My cousin placed it on a window ledge in the sunlight. The prism divided the sunlight into the beautiful colors of the rainbow. I was fascinated by the sight.

When Peter speaks of "administering God's grace in its *various* forms," the idea is of something multi-colored, like a rainbow. God's grace is one, but like the sun shining through the prism, it divides into the multicolored diversity of spiritual gifts in the Christian community. When each member ministers these gifts with holiness of life, God is glorified.

A life-style of holiness is essential for spiritual gifts to glorify God.

Holiness and Discipleship

by David E. Schroeder

THERE IS AN AGE-OLD QUERY, *What has Athens to do with Jerusalem?* that pits reason against religion. Some, in considering the relationship of holiness and discipleship, might be tempted to amend the question and ask, *What has Galilee to do with Jerusalem?*

Discipleship, they argue, relates especially to the four Gospels, written by Galileans about the earthly ministry of a Galilean, Jesus of Nazareth, whose ministry was primarily in Galilee. Holiness, on the other hand, figures more prominently in the Acts and the Letters, starting with the Upper Room in Jerusalem and the outpouring of the Holy Spirit during Pentecost.

Some others separate the terms by contending that discipleship is activity-based and holiness is an inner spiritual quality. In fact, holiness and discipleship are two sides of the same coin. Jesus brings the two together in His high priestly prayer:

> *Sanctify them [my disciples] by the truth; your word is truth. As you sent me into the world, I*

have sent them into the world. For them I sanctify myself, that they too may be truly sanctified. (John 17:17-19)

First Jesus prayed that God would sanctify His disciples by the truth. Then He stated that as God the Father had sent Him into the world, so He had sent them into the world. Finally He said that He would sanctify Himself so His disciples might be truly sanctified.

Sanctification carries two ideas: being made holy and being set apart. Sanctification means being set apart for a holy purpose. Jesus therefore prayed that His disciples would be set apart for a holy purpose, and He was setting Himself apart for a holy purpose so the disciples might also experience that same sanctification. Jesus wanted His disciples to be sanctified sent ones.

We might well argue from this text that sanctification is a prerequisite for mission. Or, in terms of our title, holiness is a prerequisite for discipleship. If that is true (and it is), why has not more been said about this relationship between the two?

Discipleship Defined

What exactly do we mean by the term *disciple*? Jesus Himself provided us a definition when He declared, "A student is not above his teacher, but everyone who is fully trained will be like his teacher" (Luke 6:40). The master/disciple relationship is a relationship of teacher to student, of instructor to novice, of craftsman to apprentice. Indeed the Greek word for disciple, *mathetes,* is the usual word for apprentice.

Interestingly, this Greek concept of teacher/student is absent from the Old Testament. There is not even an equivalent Hebrew word for *disciple*. Judaism never developed a school of Mosaism. When men called themselves "disciples of Moses" (John 9:28), they were referring to their commitment to Moses' writings, not to Moses the person.

The disinclination of the Jews to use this term stemmed from their understanding that the entire nation was under the tutelage of Yahweh, their God. Moses, for all his greatness, was merely a voice for God. There might be differing functions requiring special training, such as the levitical priesthood and the Rabbinate, but the notion that some Israelites were to be trained for a more advanced standing was foreign to their thinking. So in Rabbinate teaching, although the individual teacher had a respected role, the dominating element was the Torah.

Not Information but Commitment

In the New Testament *mathetes* occurs some 250 times, but only in the Gospels and Acts. The verbal form, *manthano*, occurs but 25 times, only 5 of them in the Gospels. This surprising disparity has a logical explanation, as Karl Rengstorf points out: The hallmark of being a disciple is *akolouthein* (to follow, obey), not merely *manthenein* (to learn). The concern of Jesus was not primarily to impart information but to awaken unconditional commitment to Himself.

Jesus personally called His disciples into a relationship with Him that demanded obedience and allegiance even to the point of suffering. Their ongoing function after His departure was to bear witness to His identity as risen Lord and Messiah. Their discipleship was not a temporary apprenticeship; it was their calling and destiny.

In the life of the early church, the term *mathetes* took on an expanded meaning to include all those committed to the lordship of Jesus Messiah. It matched *christianous* (Christians), a term probably preferred by Greek-speaking believers, for whom *mathetes* suggested the idea that Christianity was simply a philosophical movement. Indeed, it was at Antioch, where the gospel of Jesus was first preached to Greeks and "a great number of people believed and turned to the Lord," that the term *christianous* first came into use (see Acts 11:20-26).

Of Saints and Disciples

We have taken time to define New Testament discipleship. We are now ready to ask why historically the two ideas, holiness and discipleship, are not more closely aligned. Could it be that the church mistakenly has defined discipleship as Christian activity rather than commitment to the lordship of Jesus Christ?

A person becomes a new believer and someone may be available to "disciple" him or her. What does that mean? Usually it means he or she is taught to have daily personal devotions, is taught to memorize key Scriptures, is taught how to win others to Christ, is taught the importance of faithful church attendance.

We have failed to see that while Jesus gave most of His time and attention to making disciples, such things as synagogue attendance, Scripture memorization and soul-winning do not seem to have been a part of the curriculum.

Because we have a wrong understanding of discipleship, we have failed to see its relation to holiness. *Disciple,* used 250 times in the Gospels and Acts, drops out of the New Testament vocabulary after that. The writers from that point on refer to believers as "brothers," "beloved," "saints."

Paul uses the word *saint* almost 40 times. It is the Greek word *hagios,* the very word that is also translated *holy. Hagios* is the root word for *hagiosmos* (sanctification). Thus the saints are those who are sanctified.

Those called disciples in the Gospels are called saints in the Letters. Thus there is a linear continuity between discipleship and holiness. What Jesus taught about discipleship pertains also to the saints. What Paul and the other apostles taught about holiness and sanctification pertains also to discipleship.

Having established the close relationship between discipleship and holiness, we want in the rest of this chapter to focus on aspects of discipleship related to holiness and aspects of holiness that relate to discipleship. Specifically, we will see how discipleship includes separation, sanctification and devotion. And we will see how holiness encompasses Christlikeness, accountability and activism.

Discipleship and Separation

For many the essence of discipleship is separation from the world. While sanctification implies separation, separation from the world and sin is only part of it. The other part is separation to God. God never intended Christians to live in isolation. Christ's prayer for His followers (see John 17) clearly indicates His intention that they would remain in the world while living in distinction from it.

The first-century Essenes were genuinely pious. As Richard J. Cassidy points out, they believed that because of their piety the Messiah would appear exclusively to them. Surely God would not send His Anointed One to a city as corrupt as Jerusalem. But that was precisely the place where Messiah appeared. Jesus' mission was not to escape and be isolated but to invade and be involved.

That is still God's call to disciples. In the shopping mall, the high rise, the factory, the football stadium, the concert hall, the political rally, Christians can best show the contrast between God's kingdom and earthly kingdoms. Jesus very much wants Christians to be involved in the world to showcase the power of His kingdom. He prayed that God would not remove Christians from the world but protect them in the world (John 17:15).

Many Christians assume they must be separate from sinners and their society. Jesus did not live by that teaching! Nor did Paul. Paul assumed that Christians would be associated with unbelievers who were immoral, greedy, swindlers and idolaters. He *did* forbid believers from associating with so-called believers who lived like that (see 1 Corinthians 5:9-11).

To enable His disciples to live effectively in the world, Jesus taught them such qualities as flexibility, courage, compassion, trustworthiness and transparency. As disciples gain maturity in these qualities of character, they will be able to live in the world and yet not be a part of it.

Discipleship and Sanctification

A phrase that ties discipleship and sanctification together is "the lordship of Christ." Much of the debate about "lordship salvation" has generated more heat than light. Is it possible to be truly a Christian without submitting to the lordship of Jesus? In other words, may a person be "saved" only but not "sanctified"?

Without entering that debate, we may properly ask, "Why would a person even want to be a Christian without embracing the lordship of Jesus Christ?" A believer who knows Jesus as Lord of his or her life has undoubtedly experienced a crisis of sanctification and is continuing to grow in maturity through the process of sanctification. Being sanctified enables one to live effectively as a disciple because he or she is then in a right relationship with both the world and the Lord. He or she is separated from the world, separated unto the Lord.

As we noted earlier, the disciples were to be sanctified sent ones. As the saints, they were the ones Jesus prayed for and who, upon being sanctified, were then sent into the world. Discipleship and sanctification travel together. Those who are separated are sent, and those who are sent are separated.

Discipleship and Devotion

For many people the essence of holiness is adherence to a devotional way of life. Holiness for them is a matter of being faithful to a program of Bible study and prayer, commonly called devotions or the quiet time. Certainly Jesus lived devotionally with His Father and provided a model for His disciples. But apart from His training in the character qualities of discipleship, very little of His teaching seems to have focused on the development of the inner life.

Discipleship calls believers to be devoted to the Lord Jesus Christ. Devotionalism that is not devoted to Jesus Himself is merely an outward religious practice which may or may not help a Christian mature spiritually. The call to discipleship is a call to be devoted to a Person, not to the development of disciplines.

Many of the early Christians did not have devotions as we know them today. Many of them were illiterate. Even those who could read did not have access to printed Bibles. Of necessity, their devotions had to be more relational and less ritualistic. That probably was fortunate.

For us the development of holiness entails a heavy involvement with the Word of God and frequent, increasingly deeper encounters with God Himself. But a rigid discipline of Bible reading and prayer is not necessarily the only route to the goal of holiness.

Holiness and Christ-likeness

Now that we have seen how discipleship relates to various aspects of holiness, let us also see how holiness relates to three particular aspects of discipleship. We noted earlier that the essence of discipleship is becoming like one's teacher. Presumably that is where the hyphenated phrase, Christ-likeness, comes from. Jesus was totally holy. By becoming like Jesus or imitating Jesus—a con-

that Paul develops more completely in his Letters—
we enter into full discipleship and therefore holiness of life.

What does it mean to become like Jesus? Certainly we cannot take upon ourselves His physical appearance or even His personality. Becoming like
Jesus involves being conformed to His character.
The character qualities we see in Jesus are those
that we will emulate as we mature in Him. Early in
His ministry He modeled teachability, flexibility,
humility, compassion and integrity.

Later, after Peter's confession that Jesus was the
Messiah (Luke 9:18-20), Jesus became more
vigorous in His teaching of character qualities. As
He pushed the disciples on into maturity, He taught
them selflessness, intensity, courage, dependency,
trans-parency and contentment. Near the end of His
earthly ministry, Jesus stressed four final character
qualities: trustworthiness, accountability, alertness
and servanthood.

Christ-likeness also involves being "poor in
spirit," mourning, being gentle, hungering and
thirsting for righteousness, being merciful, being
pure in heart, being a peacemaker, being persecuted
for the sake of righteousness (see Matthew 5:3-10).
Matthew's Gospel adds other discipleship qualities:
brokenness, generosity, authenticity, wisdom, faithfulness. John's Gospel provides five more: love, confidence, fruitfulness, boldness, obedience.

As we saturate ourselves with the Word of God,
especially the Gospels where the character of Jesus
comes through so clearly, gaining maturity in these
qualities of character will happen almost un-
noticeably. The wonderful quality of holiness will
advance rapidly.

Holiness and Accountability

In the beginning stages of the holiness movement, John Wesley gathered believers into small groups for advancement in holy living. Wesley no doubt took his cue from Jesus, who focused most of His attention on training a small group of people. The great benefit of small group discipleship is the possibility for authentic accountability. This accountability is especially important when behavioral changes are the goal. People learn best when they know they are responsible to a peer group.

In spiritual pursuit, it is common for people either to hide in a large group or to "go it alone." Neither approach is as effective in gaining spiritual maturity as participating in a small accountability group where loving, trusting relationships can develop.

Growth in holiness, sometimes a very private matter and almost mystical, is far more likely to be successful when we are accountable to other believers. All of us have a number of blind spots. Loving, trusting brothers and sisters in Christ can point these out to us. Thus the pursuit of holiness is best accomplished in a small group setting.

Holiness and Activism

It is tempting to assume that holiness is entirely an inner, quiet attribute. Often holiness is understood more by what we do *not* do than by what we do. A strong case, however, can be made for holiness that includes a high level of Christian activism.

Jesus taught His followers that the essence of discipleship lay in their development of the character qualities we mentioned above. But He also encouraged them to follow His example of being actively engaged in the world. If we are to live Christlike lives, we may not sit on the side lines of the Christian battle. When we use the old cliche, "Christians should be 'in the world, but not of it,' " usually we are really emphasizing the latter part of the sentence, namely, that Christians are *not* to be a part of the world.

I respectfully suggest that the first part of the cliche also needs to be emphasized. Christians *are* to be in the world—meaningfully involved in the world in a redemptive way.

Christian holiness differs from what other religions consider holiness because it requires a high level of activism. Christian living allows no place for detached, monkish withdrawal from the world. We call Jesus holy because He lived a sinless life while at the same time He was very engaged in the world of humankind. Part of holiness is a life of service for others.

Conclusion

At Nyack (New York) College, where I serve as president, our motto is "Pursuing Truth; Preparing for Service." The motto would be saying the same thing if it were the title of this chapter. As Christians pursue truth ("Your Word is truth," Jesus said), they are sanctified. As they prepare for service they become disciples who in turn become disciplemakers.

This takes us back to the two great distinctives: holiness and discipleship. Two sides of the same coin.

Let's keep them together!

CHAPTER	# Holiness
24	# and
	# Persecution

by Kevin L. Walzak

HOLINESS AND PERSECUTION GO TO-GETHER. If we as believers are not being persecuted, it is either (1) the result of God's special protection or (2) the fact that we are not living lives that are holy.

We had better be especially sure it is not the latter.

Jesus warned His disciples, "If they persecuted me, they will persecute you also" (John 15:20). Paul wrote to Timothy, "Everyone who wants to live a godly life in Christ Jesus will be persecuted" (2 Timothy 3:12). Peter counseled his readers, "Do not be surprised at the painful trial you are suffering, as though something strange were happening to you. . . . If you suffer as a Christian, do not be ashamed, but praise God that you bear that name" (1 Peter 4:12, 16).

It is no coincidence that the New Testament word for witness was imported into our English language as *martyr*. Ever since Stephen (Acts 7) the two words have been linked. In Greek a witness is a *martus*. A witness stands ready to be a martyr for Jesus in whom he or she believes. Such a martyr loves Christ more than his or her own life (see Luke 14:26).

And exactly what about us Christians incites Satan's and the world's wrath? It is holiness—God's holiness as it is manifested in the world through our lives. A.W. Tozer described holiness in this way:

> Holy is the way God is. To be holy He does not conform to a standard. He is that standard. He is absolutely holy with an infinite, incomprehensible fullness of purity that is incapable of being other than it is. Because He is holy, all His attributes are holy; that is, whatever we think of as belonging to God must be thought of as holy.

To be holy is to be without evil, without fault. It is to be perfect in action, perfect in motive, perfect in every sense of the word. *Holy* implies not only sinlessness but the positive quality of being nothing but holy. Such holiness is found only in God. Some angels and some humans may share in a degree of God's holiness, but only God is completely holy.

Human beings, because of their sinfulness, are incapable of even defining true holiness apart from God's own descriptions. When we wish to define holiness, we must begin and end with God's standard as set forth in the Scriptures.

Throughout history holiness has been severely attacked by Satan and the world. Those attacks are described as *persecution*. The Scriptures record many such instances. In Hebrew the root is *radaf*, denoting the idea of pursuit with the intention of overtaking for an evil or harmful end. The Greek *dioko* can encompass several ideas, the context revealing the emphasis. Frequently the sense is of religious persecution and implies guilt on the part of the persecutor or persecutors. For example, in Philippians 3:6 Paul describes his past activity as "persecuting the church."

People Reject Both Terms

Today's church tends to reject both holiness and persecution. To speak about being holy opens a person to ridicule. Such a one is considered legalistic, uninformed or out of touch with reality. Suggest that believers reject sin in their lives, and you will be bombarded with reasons why they cannot be holy. "I'm not mature enough in my faith yet to deal with it." "God wouldn't want me to suffer like that." "I'm not ready for that yet."

Few are willing to take seriously Peter's admonition: "As obedient children, do not conform to the evil desires you had when you lived in ignorance. But just as he who called you is holy, so be holy in all you do; for it is written: 'Be holy, because I am holy' " (1 Peter 1:14-16).

As the church drifts away from a scriptural perspective of holiness, at that same time secular society is embracing unholy and distorted lifestyles. Anyone who advocates genuine holiness is regarded as weird. His or her ideas are considered absurd. I have a friend who was scorned for suggesting that no sex before marriage is the best possible advice for today's young people. The opposition, believe it or not, came from people in their 60s!

I have another friend who protested hiring an exotic dancer for their office party. He termed it ungodly and refused to have any part in it. His peers laughed at him and scorned him.

When some fellow ministers and I spoke out against pornography in our community, we drew vehement attacks from many quarters. Even the local ministerium refused to support us.

And there is the youngster who was accosted and summarily removed from the school lunch room. His flagrant violation? He had bowed his head to give thanks to God for his food.

Just as holiness is rejected by society, so persecution has come to be denied as an integral part of the Christian life. The televangelists are strangely silent on the subject. Do they see no relation between faith in Christ and persecution? At the other end of the spectrum, the advocates of "health and prosperity" seem to proliferate. If you are living a holy life, you will find smooth sailing and bounteous returns.

For the genuine Christian, holiness and persecution are integral to the pursuit of God. Anyone who makes an effort to be holy can expect opposition.

The word *Christian,* now claimed by so many that it has become nearly meaningless, began as a term of derision (Acts 11:26). *Christianous* meant "little Christs"—replicas of Jesus. The first century disciples got the epithet because they were emulating the life of their Lord and Savior. They sought to be holy in life and conduct.

Today also, a person pursuing Christ-likeness will strive to be holy—to be like Jesus. He or she will endeavor to conform to the likeness of God's Son (Romans 8:29). He or she will act the way Jesus acted, say the things Jesus would say, be in practice what Jesus would be.

We know how the world treated Jesus. Of that there can be no denial. And there can be no denial of the way those genuinely following Him were, and will be, treated. Spurgeon remarked that if the world treated the "Polished Gem" as it did, how much more will it treat in the same manner the "jewel in the rough."

In a world corrupted by sin we must realize that those unholy by nature hate anyone who exposes their sinfulness. The psalmist wrote:

> The kings of the earth take their stand
>   and the rulers gather together
> against the LORD
>   and against his Anointed One.
> "Let us break their chains," they say,
>   "and throw off their fetters." (Psalm 2:2-3)

The unholy are seeking to free themselves from the cords of God's truth. Their only means of attacking God is to attack His representatives. That is why the holy offspring of God—Christians—are under attack. They are representatives of a holy God.

Imagine a classroom of students to whom the teacher gives a surprise test. Every person but one fails the test. But that exception got a perfect score. Had it not been for that one student, the teacher explains, he would have supposed his test was too difficult. He would have adjusted all the grades upward. He would have "graded on the curve."

Will the failed students praise the one with the perfect score, congratulating her for her excellent performance? Hardly. Instead, they will be incensed and angry. Why? She exposed their failure. Her score held them accountable.

Students don't usually like curve-breakers. Curve-breakers make them work harder than they prefer to.

Jesus was a curve-breaker. He had the perfect score. His holiness exposed everyone else's failure. Instead of exalting Him, praising Him, people wanted to get Him out of their way. They killed Him. And those of His followers who set forth God's standard of righteousness can expect a similar response.

Even as holiness is a distinctive trait of the child of God, so those who do not "do what is right" are "children of the devil" (1 John 3:10). The believer must realize that children of the devil will have no love for him or her. Given the opportunity, they will vent their ferocious rebellion and hatred.

"Internal" Persecution

Often we fail to realize that this relationship between holiness and persecution applies not only externally but internally. The external persecution is obvious. We all have images of Christians being ostracized, verbally abused, even beaten, tortured and killed. Each generation has had its Stephens, its Jameses, its Pauls.

Until now, we in North America have been relatively free from open, violent persecution.

But there is "internal" persecution from which no believer is exempt. I refer to persecution by the flesh. It is essential that we understand the flesh's daily persecution upon the inner "us." If our pursuit of holiness is genuine, we must expect to be assaulted constantly by our flesh. To pursue holiness is to put to death the desires and deeds of the flesh.

Do you wonder why it is hard to pray, hard to

read your Bible, hard to pursue righteousness? It is because your flesh hates those things. It seeks to control you and to keep you from them.

If you doubt this, ask yourself where the lustful thoughts come from when you are in the midst of Bible study. Ask why you are drawn to evil even after experiencing a spiritual mountain top. *Your own flesh despises the divine nature that God has given you* (see 2 Peter 1:4).

Paul knew this truth very well. His words ring true: "I beat my body and make it my slave" (1 Corinthians 9:27). He says he gives his flesh a knockout blow in order to bring it into line. Paul was aware of the relationship between holiness and persecution. He knew that daily there would be a battle. He knew that his flesh would seek to overcome the inner man.

Some saints use the expression "dying to self." We do not put ourselves to death physically, but we say "no" to what the flesh wants and "yes" to what God wants. That is where "the rubber meets the road." Behavior and motives are shaped into holiness or unholiness depending on who gets knocked out.

The closer we get to God, the greater the flesh fights. The flesh wants nothing to do with holiness. As long as we are alive, we are not beyond falling into temptation. Only as we walk in the power of the Spirit of God can we consistently say "no" to the desires of the flesh. If we lose the battle against internal persecution, there is little hope of winning against external persecution.

A Symbiotic Relationship

One other important aspect of this relationship

between holiness and persecution needs our attention. *Persecution functions as a tool for God to use to refine us, to make us more holy.* Peter paints a picture of believers who "have had to suffer grief in all kinds of trials" (1 Peter 1:6). But he comments that this "grief" has come that their "faith—of greater worth than gold, which perishes even though refined by fire—may be proved genuine and may result in praise, glory and honor when Jesus Christ is revealed" (1:7).

Persecution is not for the purpose of showing God how much faith we have. It is for the purpose of showing *us* what we really believe and how much faith we really have. Persecution opens our eyes to the depth of our relationship with God.

Later Peter adds some further interesting information: At times it is God's will that we "suffer for doing good" (3:17). It is at such times that our obedience to the Father is being tested. Peter cites the passion of Christ. He was holy, and yet His Father saw fit to let Him experience persecution in order to fulfill His purposes. Peter's point: If Jesus was led into tribulations in order to accomplish God's purposes, we must also expect the same possibility.

It is a great tester of faith to trust God amid persecution. But that is the crux of the battle: to be obedient even when things aren't pleasant. Our willingness to be obedient at such times is an indication of genuine faith. It means we have said "yes" to the holy desires of God and "no" to the unholy desires of our flesh.

Persecution is a part of God's refining process. With valuable metals there must be intense heat to remove the impurities. If those metals could talk, they'd be protesting the furnace vociferously. But afterward, they would never want to go back to their old impure state.

Throughout the Scriptures we see the principle: God raises up opposition to purge evil and evil ones from among His people. It was true of Israel during the days of the judges and the kingdom. It has not changed. "God disciplines us for our good, that we may share in his holiness. No discipline seems pleasant at the time, but painful. Later on, however, it produces a harvest of righteousness and peace for those who have been trained by it" (Hebrews 12:10-11).

Note two important points: First, God "disciplines those he loves, / and he punishes everyone he accepts as a son" (Hebrews 12:6). No real Christian will be excluded from God's woodshed. Second, God does it "that we may share in His holiness" (12:10). How exciting it is to know that God, as a result of His discipline, that often comes in the form of persecution, is producing holy fruit in our lives!

Holiness and persecution clearly are related. Holiness is uniquely God's attribute: we are holy only by being linked to God through Jesus Christ. That very God-quality of holiness incites Satan's fury and that of all his followers. "The son born in the ordinary way persecuted the son born by the power of the Spirit" (Galatians 4:29). It is a spiritual battle.

Three centuries of relatively little outward persecution in North America have produced a flabby generation of Christians who have lost the correct perspective of holiness and rejected persecution as integral to the Christian life.

Whatever our persecution from the outside, we can expect opposition from the flesh—internal persecution. There is a battle in every believer between the flesh and the spirit. Just as the world and the devil try to overtake and mistreat those pursuing and propagating holiness, in the same way the true believer who pursues holiness is constantly being assaulted by the flesh. To pursue holiness is to put to death the desires and deeds of the flesh.

Persecution is not all bad. There is, in fact, a symbiotic relationship between the two. Genuine holiness in the believer draws persecution from the devil, the world and the flesh. At the same time, persecution can produce holiness in the believer to overcome the flesh, the world and Satan.

Only a fool would say that he or she wants to be persecuted. But I fear we have moved beyond such a concept. We have embraced a diabolical deception: *Only the foolish are persecuted.* We have forgotten some of Jesus' words:

> *Blessed are those who are persecuted because*
> *of righteousness,*
> *for theirs is the kingdom of heaven.*
> *Blessed are you when people insult you, persecute you and falsely say all kinds of evil against you because of me.* (Matthew 5:10-11)

Tragically, in the peace and safety of our generation we have faltered on the main battle front. In practice we have embraced the desires of the flesh and called them "holy." We now suppose that only the foolish would die to self and deny the things of this world. Only a fool would waste his or her life on a mission field. Only a fool would leave a "great" career to teach at a seminary or pastor a church. Only a fool would work harder to give more for the spread of the gospel.

The indictment of such statements pierces us all. In the inner battle the flesh has conquered many a Christian's conscience and deceived him or her into thinking godliness is the pursuit of life, liberty and happiness—above death, holiness and sacrifice.

Just as genuine holiness draws persecution, at the same time persecution can strengthen our holy resolve to overcome the flesh, the world and the devil. Jesus said: "Do not suppose that I have come to bring peace to the earth. I did not come to bring peace, but a sword" (Matthew 10:34). Until we meet Jesus, holiness and persecution will be uniquely intertwined.

[God] is not only the pattern [for holy living], but the Source. His holiness is the guarantee of ours. He commands because He gives what He commands. Out of His fullness we receive. We shine in His reflected light, even as the planets shine in the light of the great day star.
—A.B. Simpson—

The Holy Family

by George S. Liebmann

A S A COLLEGE STUDENT, I had the good fortune of landing a work-scholarship as host in the climate-controlled comfort of a large gallery of sacred art right on the campus. Paintings by the old masters depicted many themes, but one theme was dominant. The gallery collection was heavily weighted with paintings of the Holy Family.

That gallery was a kind of Holy Family album somewhat like the album of snapshots on your coffee table. I feel I know the Holy Family better for having spent many hours browsing among those paintings.

Those masterpieces were the products of the painters' imaginations. For a completely accurate depiction of the Holy Family, we must turn to the prose painting found in Luke 2:39-52:

> When Joseph and Mary had done everything required by the Law of the Lord, they returned to Galilee to their own town of Nazareth. And the child grew and became strong; he was filled with

wisdom, and the grace of God was upon him.

Every year his parents went to Jerusalem for the Feast of the Passover. When he was twelve years old, they went up to the Feast, according to the custom. After the Feast was over, while his parents were returning home, the boy Jesus stayed behind in Jerusalem, but they were unaware of it. Thinking he was in their company, they traveled on for a day. Then they began looking for him among their relatives and friends. When they did not find him, they went back to Jerusalem to look for him. After three days they found him in the temple courts, sitting among the teachers, listening to them and asking them questions. Everyone who heard him was amazed at his understanding and his answers. When his parents saw him, they were astonished. His mother said to him, "Son, why have you treated us like this? Your father and I have been anxiously searching for you."

"Why were you searching for me?" he asked. "Didn't you know I had to be in my Father's house?" But they did not understand what he was saying to them.

Then he went down to Nazareth with them and was obedient to them. But his mother treasured all these things in her heart. And Jesus grew in wisdom and stature, and in favor with God and men.

Complete Obedience to God

The first thing we notice in this portrait of the Holy Family is that Joseph and Mary did "everything required by the Law of the Lord." It may not have been easy or convenient. For a family of very modest means it was barely affordable. But they complied fully with the Mosaic Law. *Radical, complete obedience to God* was at the heart of their parenting philosophy.

As a consequence of this God-first philosophy, "the child grew and became strong; he was filled with wisdom, and the grace of God was upon him." Living in obedience to God's commands is the healthiest life-style possible. Who knows better than the Creator how to nurture, strengthen and preserve human life? God's Word is an "owner's manual," a set of "Manufacturer's instructions" for the operation and maintenance of the human spirit, soul and body. Life works better when we pay attention!

Not only was there physical well-being, but the child Jesus was "filled with wisdom." Wisdom is precious. It usually is the result of living long through many mistakes. But because the family's obedience was consistent, God filled Jesus with wisdom when He was only a child.

There was yet another result of the Holy Family's obedience: God put His evident grace upon the growing child. Certainly this is the greatest of the gifts bestowed on the holy. To fully appreciate its value we must go beyond the generic definition of grace as unmerited favor and think of it as *the desire and ability to do God's will*. This desire was evident in 12-year-old Jesus when He declared , "Didn't you know I had to be in my Father's house?"

Coupled with this desire to do God's will was ability. Luke comments, "Everyone . . . was amazed at his understanding and his answers."

What Obedience Does *Not* Spare Us From

The incident in the temple courts is a reminder to

us that complete obedience to God, while desirable, does not automatically spare us from life's normal problems. For Joseph and Mary, their obedience to God's Law did not prevent moments of anxiety, uncertainty, even frustration. We hear it in Mary's words: "Son, why have you treated us like this? Your father and I have been anxiously searching for you." No philosophy of parenting, however sound, will eliminate all the anxiety, uncertainty and frustration.

Luke's comment is instructive: "They did not understand what he was saying to them." One of my children has a T-shirt that says, "Don't try to understand me—just love me." It fits her to a T in more ways than one! Shelves of books have been written to help parents understand their children. While being able to "understand" our children is helpful, understanding is not the bottom line to successful parenting. Holiness manifested in obedience is the bottom line.

Although full obedience did not communicate total understanding or eliminate anxiety, uncertainty and frustration, it did continue to produce a number of excellent, desirable rewards.

The Rewards of Complete Obedience

The first reward we find here was—more obedience! Luke relates that after Mary and Joseph had found Jesus "in the temple courts, sitting among the teachers, he went down to Nazareth with them and was obedient to them." We cannot expect to reap obedience in our children if we do not sow the seeds of obedience to our Heavenly Father. It is not obedience commanded or demanded that produces more obedience, but obedience modeled.

Good memories were another reward of complete obedience. "His mother treasured all these things in her heart." Families *will* produce memories, but not all memories are created equal. Families characterized by disobedience produce haunting, debilitating, painful memories. Holy families have the capacity to produce memories that are lifetime treasures.

There was a third reward for complete obedience. It was a Child who "grew in wisdom and stature, and in favor with God and men." Here is well-rounded growth—intellectual, vocational, physical, spiritual and social. What parent would not be delighted by results like that!

Is the Holy Family a Problem?

Truly this was a Holy Family. But for some of us that Holy Family may be a problem. In our own parenting struggles, how can we relate to a mother with a halo, to a father who heard from angels, to a Baby who glows quietly amid treasures of gold, frankincense and myrrh? Can a family that is not *the* Holy Family be *a* holy family? Does the Bible tell us about any *ordinary* holy families and how they got that way?

An Old Testament prophet—Jeremiah, of all people—has an answer for us. The Lord commanded Jeremiah to invite "the whole family of the Recabites" (Jeremiah 35:3) to a room off the temple court. There he was to offer them wine to drink.

Even though the wine was offered in obedience to the Lord by the Lord's prophet in the Lord's house, the Recabites refused it. Their explanation:

> *We do not drink wine, because our forefather Jonadab son of Recab gave us this command: "Neither you nor your descendants must ever drink wine. Also you must never build houses, sow seed or plant vineyards; you must note have any of these things, but must always live in tents. Then you will live a long time in the land where you are nomads."*
>
> *We have obeyed everything our forefather Jonadab son of Recab commanded us. Neither we nor our wives nor our sons and daughters have ever drunk wine or built houses to live in or had vineyards, fields or crops. We have lived in tents and have fully obeyed everything our forefather Jonadab commanded us.* (Jeremiah 35:6-10).

I am not sure what the attitude of contemporary Christians would be to instructions of an ancestor, dead two centuries, who circumscribed what they could drink, where they could live and how they could earn a living. With the exception of the Amish, most modern Christian families would consider this kind of obedience extreme.

But What Did God Think?

We are not left to wonder what God thought about all of this. Hear Jeremiah again:

> *This is what the LORD Almighty, the God of Israel, says: "You have obeyed the command of your forefather Jonadab and have followed everything he ordered. . . . Jonadab son of Recab will never fail to have a man to serve me."* (35:18-19)

When God finds someone who really understands

the vital importance of radical, complete obedience, He wants that person on His team! And although we may not have any instructions for our life-style handed down from our ancestors, our Heavenly Father has given us detailed principles and precepts on which we can practice obedience in our families—with similar results.

If you like those results, if you want to be a holy family, if you are willing to commit to radical, complete obedience fleshed out in your own home, the Bible has further help for you. In Deuteronomy 6:1-9 the Bible offers instruction that Jewish holy families followed, both in Old Testament times and New. These instructions are equally effective for contemporary Christian families who desire that same level of holiness and its rewards.

God gave these instructions, Moses told Israel, "so that you, your children and their children after them may fear the LORD your God as long as you live by keeping all his decrees and commands that I give you, and so that you may enjoy long life" (Deuteronomy 6:2).

Right Actions, Right Motives

Right actions only qualify as holiness when they flow from right motives. God begins with love: "Love the LORD your God with all your heart and with all your soul and with all your strength" (6:5). Fear may motivate the immature, but for the mature, love must be the motivation to obedience. Love produces obedience from the heart—soulful, strong obedience that not only delights in the best of times but is willing to bear a cross in the worst. One of the great joys of the holy family is to watch our children mature from inconsistent obedience motivated by fear to a love-motivated desire to honor God.

All obedience, even mature obedience, must be informed. If it is to honor and please God, it must be given direction. And God has made provision for this. All the direction we need for holy living is between the covers of our Bibles. But if that is where it stays, it does us little good. God says, "These commandments that I give you today are to be upon your hearts" (6:6).

The result of God's Word moving from Bible to our hearts is as the psalmist testified: "I have hidden your word in my heart / that *I might not sin* against you" (Psalm 119:11, emphasis added). The spiritual disciplines of study and meditation are the beginning of holiness in the heart first, then the home.

Enter the Holy Spirit

If it is to make us holy, God's Word must move from Bible to heart. And if God's commandments are to make our family holy, we must make a point to "impress them on [our] children" (Deuteronomy 6:7).

This is a good time to remind ourselves that apart from the Holy Spirit there can be no holy person and no holy family. Even if we could love God without the aid of the Holy Spirit (we can't), even if we could internalize God's revelation without the Spirit of Truth (again, we can't), we would still need the aid of the Holy Spirit to impress God's Word on our children.

It is imperative that I put within the hearts of my children the principles and precepts of God. How I need the Holy Spirit's help in this task! The Spirit tells me how to do it: "Talk about [my commandments] when you sit at home and when you walk along the road, when you lie down and when you get up. Tie them as symbols on your hands and bind them on your foreheads. Write them on the doorframes of your houses and on your gates" (6:7-9).

Do you understand what the Spirit is saying? An hour of Sunday school once a week will not produce a holy family. The instruction your children get at church can and should reinforce your teaching. But if the Word is to make an effective impression, they must hear it taught and see it lived in a Monday-through-Saturday context.

Two Questions

In any discussion of a holy family, two questions come to mind. The first: *Will the requisite radical obedience require a major change of lifestyle?* Quite possibly. Real Christianity (interpret that *holiness*) is not a bolt-on option to the North American Dream. Most families will need to break the mold and retool. Holiness is a distinct lifestyle, rooted in the priority of our relationship with Jesus over any other goal or ambition.

The second question: *Will it work?* If I, one individual before God, commit to radical obedience, will I be assured of a holy family and its attendant blessings?

In First Corinthians 7:13-15 Paul isolates what I regard as the "worst case scenario" in parenting. A believing wife or husband occupies the same living space with an unbelieving spouse. Single parenting is difficult in many ways, but think of the inevitable clash of values when the unbelieving partner clash of values when the unbelieving partner chooses to stay! And what does Paul say? "The unbelieving husband has been sanctified through his wife, and the unbelieving wife has been sanctified through her believing husband. Otherwise your children would be unclean, but as it is, *they are holy*" (emphasis added). If it works in the worst of cases, it should work in all cases!

Certainly this is a precious promise to the embattled mother or father who lacks spousal support and who even may endure opposition as she or he struggles to develop a holy family.

God knows your situation. *He* is holy. Holiness flows from Him. It can flow through you into your family like it flowed through Jonadab, like it flowed through Joseph and Mary.

Purpose to be a holy family. Commit to radical, complete obedience. Then watch God's health, wisdom and grace flow into your home through the Sanctifier Himself.

The union with Christ is so complete that He imparts His own nature to us, and lives His own life in us. . . . We live Christ-like lives because we have the Christ life.
—A.B. Simpson—

	Holiness
CHAPTER	in the
26	Family

by Joy Jacobs

THE LONGER I STUDY THE Bible, the more strongly I believe that God provided examples of human relationships in the Bible for our instruction and spiritual development.

Let's think about Abraham. His name originally was Abram. His seemingly unwavering trust in God is referred to in Romans 4, Hebrews 11 and James 2. Abraham, his son Isaac and his grandson Jacob are all cited in the "Hall of Fame of Faith," Hebrews 11. Without doubt, all three patriarchs had a heart for God. They were special in His sight.

Note how God promises blessing to all three. He said to Abraham, "Because you have . . . not withheld your son, your only son, I will surely bless you . . . and through your offspring all nations on earth will be blessed, because you have obeyed me" (Genesis 22:16–18).

Years later God said to Isaac: "Do not be afraid, for I am with you; I will bless you and will increase the number of your descendants" (26:24).

To Jacob God said: "I am the LORD, the God of your father Abraham and the God of Isaac. . . . I am

with you and will watch over you wherever you go.
. . . I will not leave you until I have done what I
have promised you" (28:13-15).

They, Too, Were Humanly Flawed

These wonderful pronouncements tend to leave
us with the impression that the patriarchs of the
faith never stepped away from holy ground. But
there were two sides to their lives.

I am not suggesting they were Jekyll/Hyde personalities or even hypocritical. No, each of them
truly had a heart for God. But each of them was also
humanly flawed, just as we are.

Perhaps one of the reasons we prefer to think of
Bible characters as different is—well, it's easier that
way. Surely they had to be superhuman to be able
to do the things God asked of them!

Obviously, we are *not* superhuman, so God can't
expect us to give up a beloved only child as
Abraham did, or entrust the choice of a wife to a
servant, as Isaac did, or wait seven years for the wife
he loved, as Jacob did.

"I could never do that," we say to God. "I'm too
ordinary, too human." And we tell ourselves that's a
good reason to excuse ourselves from a difficult assignment.

But as I studied the family of Abraham, I had to
conclude that its members were *very* human. In fact,
they are classic examples of many of the problems we
see in family relationships today. In particular, they
exemplify three relationship patterns:

• the need for control, the need for self-
protection

- a lack of, or breakdown in, communication
- an inability to handle conflict in a God-honoring way

All in the Family

If we look at Abraham's family tree, we discover that Abram and Sarai (as she was then known) had the same father—Terah—but different mothers. Thus Sarai was Abram's half-sister. They may well have remained with their father Terah in the family home in Ur of the Chaldees. From what archaeologists tell us, it may have been a beautiful place, perhaps a two-storied, balconied house, with silky oriental rugs gracing its tiled floors. Sarai may have had servants to dress her, to prepare her food and of course to care for the housekeeping chores.

That Sarai was beautiful we know. We also know she was childless. In that culture, giving one's husband an heir was the most meaningful part of a woman's life, if not her only claim to significance. Sarai married her 10-year-older "big brother," whom she had known and trusted all her life. It is also possible he treated her as the child she had been when he became a man.

At some point—we are not told when or why—Terah determined to move to Canaan, a relatively primitive area far to the west of Ur. Is it possible that God first called *Terah* to leave country and kindred and "go to the land I will show you" (Genesis 12:1)? We do not know. We know that Abram and Sarai and other family members set out with him. We also know that Terah stopped midway, settling in Haran.

Abram was 75, Sarai was 65 when God's call came

to Abram in Haran: "Leave your country, your people and your father's household and go to the land I will show you" (Genesis 12:1). Although he and Sarai still had no children, God promised He would make Abram into "a great nation." (12:2).

"Wait for Me! I'm Your Wife!"

Sarai's name, according to some commentators, meant *contentious*. Perhaps Sarai had never had reason to question Abram's complete control. What was her response now? Did Abram *really* communicate with Sarai? Did he take time for her uneasy, perhaps unsettling questions? Did they pray together about this major decision of their lives?

God's move-out message to Abram involved innumerable personal sacrifices for Sarai, who was still so beautiful that she became a threat to her husband's safety. Abram's seeming tendency to control without prayerful discussion or thought about the consequences brought both of them into a compromising situation.

Just how long they had been in Canaan we are not told, but a severe famine prompted Abram to move temporarily to Egypt. Fearing the Egyptians might kill him in order to acquire his beautiful wife, Abram instructed Sarai to say she was his sister.

Neither of them had imagined it would be the king himself who would take an interest in Sarai. Abram was indeed treated well, very well, but if God had not intervened, Pharaoh would have had Sarai, and Abram would have returned to Canaan wealthier but wife-less.

What feelings did Abram's deceit and self-protection arouse in Sarai? Perhaps a bit of pride that she was still considered a beauty, but certainly not a feeling of being protected or valued by her husband! From that point on, Sarai's feelings of betrayal and abandonment, it seems, left her resentful and somewhat demanding, even illogical at times.

Giving God a Little Help

By age 75 Sarai—quite understandably—had given up on God's promise of a child, much less a great nation. She ordered Abram to sleep with her maidservant, Hagar, in hopes of becoming at least a surrogate mother to Hagar's child.

Abram agreed (no argument is recorded!) and Hagar conceived. Immediately Hagar began to act arrogantly—and just as quickly Sarai reacted to Hagar's contempt. She turned to Abram.

"You are responsible for the wrong I am suffering" (Genesis 16:5), Sarai said accusingly. (Whose idea was it?) Then she added an expression of hostility and suspicion: "May the Lord judge between you and me."

And how did Abram handle conflict? It seems he failed to take responsibility in this "blended family." Instead, he sat back passively, giving Sarai permission to do whatever she pleased. And Sarai, in this particular situation, did *not* evidence "the unfading beauty of a gentle and quiet spirit" (1 Peter 3:4). Sarai mistreated Hagar, so much so that Hagar fled into the desert.

Since Abram was passive, God stepped in. Not only did "the God who sees" make a spring of water available to Hagar, but He sent His angel to encourage her. Think of it! God took time to provide water and a guardian angel for a slave girl! Hagar knew she had an Advocate.

And so did Abram. Isn't it encouraging to realize that after all those years of human mistakes and failures, God came to Abram again? By then Abram was 99 and Sarai was 89. To both of them God reaffirmed His promises. God even changed their names to Abraham (meaning *father of many nations*) and Sarah (meaning *princess*) to emphasize the way in which their lives would change.

The Promise Renewed

It's interesting that God renewed His promises to Abraham in a setting where Sarah could hear God's voice as well. Might it have been because He couldn't trust Abraham to communicate with his wife? God said, "I will surely return to you about this time next year, and Sarah your wife will have a son" (Genesis 18:10).

Can you imagine the joy Sarah felt when she discovered she was finally pregnant—at age 89?

Abraham was 100 when Isaac was born. Both Abraham and Sarah had laughed in disbelief when in their old age God promised them a son. Now, perhaps, they finally laughed together. Isaac's name meant *laughter*.

Without doubt, Isaac immediately became his mother's delight—and her identity as well. He had finally given her life meaning and significance. Did he become a "mama's boy"? Did he draw even closer to his mother after the sacrificial pilgrimage he and his father made to Mount Moriah? Did Abraham teach his wife and son the ways of God? Did he take time to interpret God's messages to his family? Such questions cannot be answered absolutely from the Scriptures. We do know, however, that God is very specific in His job description for fathers. They are to impress God's commands on their children, to "talk about them when you sit at home and when you walk along the road, when you lie down and when you get up" (Deuteronomy 6:7).

Like Father, Like Son

It is interesting that Isaac did not take a wife until after his mother's death. After Sarah died, Abraham remarried. He had another six sons by Keturah, his new wife. How did Keturah and six more sons affect Abraham's relationship with Isaac?

Isaac was 40 years old (Genesis 25:20) when Abraham sent his servant Eliezer to look for a bride for Isaac. Eliezer brought back the beautiful Rebekah. Isaac welcomed her, the Bible says (Genesis 24:66–67). But after Isaac had been his mother's pride and joy for 37 years, did Rebekah ever feel she could fill Sarah's sandals? Did she and Isaac learn to communicate with each other?

Patterns are powerful, especially patterns in relationships! To our horror, we see in Genesis 26 Isaac recycling Dad's deceit. Just like his father, Isaac tried to pass off Rebekah as his sister. Except that Rebekah was *not* his sister! Not even his half-sister.

How must Rebekah have felt? The result may well have been a wounded spirit, possibly a closed spirit—to her husband and perhaps to God.

After years of waiting for a child, Isaac and Rebekah finally had twin boys, Jacob and Esau. Sadly, each parent picked a favorite—and then formed coalitions against each other. Finally, the breakdown in communication and the inability to handle conflict led once again to deceit—manipulation and lying. Yes, God had promised that the elder (Esau) would serve the younger (Jacob). But Rebekah and Jacob deceived blind old Isaac to ensure that Rebekah's favorite would receive the blessing. Certainly God didn't need their help to achieve His purpose!

There Is More to Come

The saga continues. Esau threatened Jacob's life, and Jacob ran away to the home of Laban, back in Haran. There Jacob, in turn, was deceived by Laban, his uncle. Jacob bargained for Laban's good-looking daughter Rachel. The wife Laban gave him was his older daughter Leah. Later we see Laban's younger daughter, Rachel (whom Jacob also married) playing the same old game of deceit with Dad.

Esau, back home in Canaan, knew that his mother Rebekah was bitter about the heathen Canaanite women he had married. In an effort to please his parents, Esau took another wife—Mahaloth, the granddaughter of Hagar, the daughter of Ishmael.

Who had won in the battle for control? No one! Communication in Isaac and Rebekah's marriage broke down long before the family broke apart. They were unable to handle conflict constructively.

In Abraham and his extended family we see:

• *Abraham's self-protection passed down to Isaac, his son.* It sorely wounded Sarah; it most certainly wounded the spirit of Rebekah, who retaliated with manipulation and deceit that resulted in the family's breakup.

• *Abraham's apparent poor communication with Sarah passed down to Isaac, and from Isaac to Esau and Jacob.* Family members who once loved each other became isolated.

• *Abraham's inability to handle conflict in a God-honoring way passed on to Isaac and to Jacob and Esau, setting the scene for Joseph's ill treatment by his brothers.* When Abraham gave in to Sarah concerning her treatment of Hagar he began a conflict that continues to this day. Isaac and Ishmael are still fighting!

Some of these very human people had a heart for God. May we be able to learn from their mistakes. God loved them in spite of their faults. And God loves us in spite of ours.

David Seamands, writing in *Healing for Damaged Emotions,* says, "Grace is the face God wears when He meets our imperfections, sin, weakness and failure."

But, as the Bible asks in Romans 6:1, "Shall we go on sinning so that grace may increase?" The Bible answers its own question: "By no means!" Whereas sin once controlled us, we should now offer ourselves to God "as those who have been brought from death to life" (Romans 6:13).

In Nathaniel Hawthorne's *The Scarlet Letter,* an adulteress was forced to wear the letter *A* on her dress so that everyone would be aware of her sin. Had the practice been current in Bible times, perhaps some of Abraham's family would have worn the letter *D* for *deceit.* (See chart, "Recycling Family Patterns.")

Open your heart to God and ask Him, "What let-

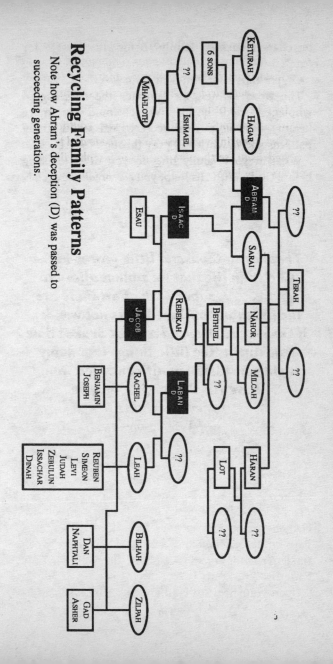

Recycling Family Patterns

Note how Abram's deception (D) was passed to succeeding generations.

ter characterizes *my* family? *B* for *bitterness*? *F* for *fear*?

Or, perhaps *P* for *prayer* or *L* for *love*!

The word *holiness* incorporates the meaning of wholeness and health. What could be more healthy—and holy—than to recognize sinful family patterns and to work and pray through them?

What in your family line do you need to bring before God? With His help, *you can break the cycle!*

There are a thousand little graces in the Christian life that we cannot afford to ignore. . . . In any work of art there are the finishing touches. Let us not wonder if God seems to spend a great deal of time teaching us the little things that many might consider insignificant. God would have His Bride without spot or even wrinkle.

—A.B. Simpson—

Holiness Across Culture

by Angel V. Ortiz

CULTURAL DIVERSITY HAS BECOME IN the United States a predominant, "political-ly correct" term. Newscasters, talk show hosts and commentators are pressing it to its limit. The supposition is that cultural diversity and in-dividualism are the factors that explain the uniqueness and strength of American society.

This mind-set, strangely enough, has also invaded American churches. It should not have done so. God declares of the church:

> *Once you were not a people, but now you are the people of God; once you had not received mercy, but now you have received mercy.* (1 Peter 2:10)

Again, the Bible proclaims:

> *[God] chose us in [Jesus Christ] before the creation of the world to be holy and blameless in his sight.* (Ephesians 1:4)

Both references are to the church, the *ecclesia*, the

"called-out ones." The people of God are a people who have been called out of the world and set apart unto God. They are the ones called to be holy and blameless in God's sight. Throughout the centuries, holiness has been the identifying mark of the people of God.

Those who comprise the visible body of Jesus Christ, historically committed to the building up of each other, now suddenly have been replaced by a collection of individuals who idolize both their "cultural diversity" and their own particular gifts.

Holiness, once the distinguishing and unifying factor in the church, has been set aside for the glamour of individuality.

Let's Get Back to the Church

Much of the present teaching on holiness and sanctification has centered on the personal experiences of individual believers. As a result, the broader aspects of the doctrine as it relates to God's people collectively in the church have been overlooked, if not deliberately ignored.

If we are to regard as of importance the practical teaching of the Bible, then holiness must be presented in the context of the church as the whole body of Christ. The Scriptures go on to say:

> There should be no division in the body, but . . .
> its parts should have equal concern for each other.
> If one part suffers, every part suffers with it; if one
> part is honored, every part rejoices with it.
> (1 Corinthians 12:25-26)

By a divine work of grace, the Spirit of God regenerates repentant sinners. The Bible describes the transformation: "If anyone is in Christ, he is a new creation; the old has gone, the new has come!" (2 Corinthians 5:17). This divine work of the Spirit of God does more than save the individual sinner. It makes that former sinner a part of the called-out ones, the holy people. It is therefore plain to see that holiness is more than the positional privilege of the believer in Christ Jesus (1 Corinthians 1:30). It is more than the sanctifying work of the Holy Spirit in his or her life (2 Thessalonians 2:13-14). It is also the visible, detectable characteristic that has always marked the people of God, no matter what their culture.

The Hispanic Church Is an Example

There is no better example of holiness across culture than the Hispanic church in North America. Both the United States and Canada possess an unusual magnetism when it comes to attracting people from other nations of the world. As a result, they have become immense depositories of people from various nations, languages and cultures.

The Hispanics who have flocked to the borders of the United States and migrated into the nation have come from many countries and diverse cultural backgrounds. Once in the United States, they are drawn together by two factors: They are in a foreign country, and they speak Spanish. Besides those two factors, they are as different as English-speaking people who might originate in England or India or the Philippines.

When one of the Hispanic churches meets for worship, you may find people from Mexico, Puerto Rico, Cuba, Colombia, Peru, Guatemala, El Salvador, Venezuela, the United States or any of the other Latin American countries, including the Caribbean. Although they share a common heritage and language, they are noticeably diverse in culture. But when they meet for worship, there is a commonality that unites them. It is a commonality not dependent on language or the fact that they are in a foreign country. This commonality is a divine awareness that *they are a separated people* with a *heavenly citizenship* and a marked characteristic: *holy*.

Culture, by definition, draws people into a standard of commonality and identity. Holiness breaks through the external implications of culture, piercing to the internal needs of lives, transforming them, giving them new values, new purpose, new identity. They are enabled to achieve *unity amid the diversity* of cultures, languages and traditionals.

A Chosen People

From the beginning, the Lord has sought for those who would be separated from the world around them and set apart for Him.

Enoch comes to mind. Enoch "walked with God 300 years" (Genesis 5:22). This visible expression of the holiness of Enoch is also described in Hebrews 11:5 by the words, "one who pleased God."

Noah lived a life different from those around him. The Bible describes him as one who "found favor in the eyes of the LORD" (Genesis 6:8) and as "a righteous man, blameless among the people of his time" (6:9). Faith (internal reality) and righteousness (an external, identifying mark) characterized

Noah (Hebrews 11:7).

Abraham was called by God to leave his kin for a new land. "By faith [internal reality again] he made his home in the promised land like a stranger in a foreign country" (Hebrews 11:9). God promised to make from him a great nation that would bless all the peoples of the earth. Thus Abraham and his household chose to become a separated people, holy (the external identifying mark again) unto the Lord (Genesis 12:1-3).

Melchizedek, king of Salem, stood out among the people of Canaan. The Scriptures describe him as "priest of God Most High" (Genesis 14:18).

Jacob, Moses, Samuel, Ezra

Jacob, renamed Israel, was given confirmation by God that His divine purpose for the people of Israel would outwardly demonstrate a separation from the ways of the other nations around them (Genesis 35:1-4, 9-12). Jacob was very much aware that he and his people were to be separated unto the Lord.

Moses was called to lead the nation Israel out from Egyptian bondage. The people of Israel lived separated from the Egyptians in the land of Goshen (Genesis 47:1-6), receiving direct blessing and protection from God.

Later, through Moses, God explained to the nation why He had chosen to bring Israel out of Egypt:

> *You yourselves have seen what I did to Egypt, and how I carried you on eagles' wings and brought you to myself. Now if you obey me fully and keep my covenant, then out of all nations you*

283

*will be my treasured possession. Although the
whole earth is mine, you will be for me a kingdom
of priests and a holy nation.* (Exodus 19:4-6)

Samuel the prophet contended with the people of
Israel because they wanted to be "like all the other
nations" around them instead of being holy unto
the Lord (1 Samuel 8:20). The people prevailed and
got their king—to their sorrow.

Ezra the priest confronted the remnant that
returned from captivity with their obvious lack of
separation from the heathen nations who held
them. In their own land, too, they had not remained
separate: "The leaders came to me and said, 'The
people of Israel, including the priests and the
Levites, have not kept themselves separate from the
neighboring people with their detestable practices.
. . . They have . . . mingled the holy race with the
peoples around them' " (Ezra 9:1-2).

These and many other Old Testament examples
reveal that God has been interested not only in the
inward experience of holiness but also in the outward result of that holiness as it manifested itself in
the lives of those it transformed. He seeks for a
separated people!

The Mystery of Holiness across Culture

As we enter the revelation of God's word and will
in the New Testament, we are introduced to the
"mystery" of Christ, not made known theretofore:

> *This mystery is that through the gospel the Gen-
> tiles [across culture] are heirs together with Is-
> rael, members together of one body, and sharers*

together in the promise in Christ Jesus. . . . Although I [Paul] am less than the least of all God's people, this grace was given me: to preach to the Gentiles the unsearchable riches of Christ, and to make plain to everyone the administration of this mystery, which for ages past was kept hidden in God, who created all things. His intent was that now, through the church, the manifold wisdom of God should be made known to the rulers and authorities in the heavenly realms, according to his eternal purpose which he accomplished in Christ Jesus our Lord. (Ephesians 3:6-11)

God's eternal purpose accomplished in Christ Jesus was *the church!* Not only was Israel to be a separated people, holy unto the Lord, but also the Gentiles were to become in Christ Jesus a separated people demonstrating holiness inwardly and outwardly.

The Bible declares, "You are all sons of God through faith in Christ Jesus, for all of you who were baptized into Christ have clothed yourselves with Christ. There is neither Jew nor Greek, slave nor free, male nor female, for you are all one in Christ Jesus. If you belong to Christ, then you are Abraham's seed, and heirs according to the promise" (Galatians 3:26-29).

A Message for All People

The call of holiness proclaimed by Peter reveals that it is a message for all people: "To God's elect, strangers in the world, scattered . . ." (1 Peter 1:1). It is a call to live lives outwardly separated from the ways of the world: "As obedient children, do not conform to the evil desires you had when you lived in ignorance. But just as he who called you is holy, so be holy in all you do; for it is written: 'Be holy, because I am holy' " (1:14-16).

Most of all, it is a call to the unifying effects of a separated people from across cultures:

> You are a chosen people, a royal priesthood, a holy nation, a people belonging to God, that you may declare the praises of him who called you out of darkness into his wonderful light. Once you were not a people, but now you are the people of God; once you had not received mercy, but now you have received mercy. (2:9-10)

Holiness across culture is more than a message to the individual believer. It is a message to the whole body of Christ. It is the identifying mark of the people of God. It is the unifying factor of believers from all languages, tribes and nations.

> After this I looked and there before me was a great multitude that no one could count, from every nation, tribe, people and language, standing before the throne and in front of the Lamb. They were wearing white robes and were holding palm branches in their hands. And they cried out in a loud voice:

> "Salvation belongs to our God,
> who sits on the throne,
> and to the Lamb." (Revelation 7:9-10)

Holiness and the Gray Areas

by William R. Goetz

CAN CHRISTIANS ATTEND THE THEATER, engage in social drinking, dance, watch TV indiscriminately and listen to modern music? Or are these—and many similar activities—sinful? After all, the Bible doesn't really say anything *specifically* about any of the above.

Not too many years ago evangelical pastors and churches throughout North America had very strong attitudes toward activities like theater-going, dancing, social drinking and so on. Those things were, without question, "worldly." For believers they were strictly taboo.

Pastors often very clearly and forcefully verbalized these taboos. They devoted whole sermons to pointing out the "sinfulness" and "dangers" of such things. Admittedly, there was a good amount of legalism mixed in with their methods and manner of opposing such "sins."

I'm dead set against legalism. I want absolutely no part of it. But on the other hand, I find myself deeply disturbed by the fact that today in evangelical circles we have gone to the other extreme. In our reaction to legalism we appear to be dangerously close to license.

Many who profess to be Bible-believing Christians from a wide variety of churches have no qualms whatever (in their "Christian liberty") about engaging in many of the things previously categorized as "sin." For example:

- theater attendance
- "harmless" social drinking
- watching movies on TV
- indiscriminate watching of commercial videos
- dancing
- listening to rock music, Christian and secular

The list could go on into the areas of fashions, reading habits, smoking and so on.

What's the Answer?

What is the answer? Can we avoid legalism and yet find a solid biblical way to know what is right or wrong? Can we find our way through the maze of options before us to the path of genuine holiness?

Let's look at it this way. In God's Word there are a great many things that Christians, if they wish to be obedient children of God, are specifically commanded or encouraged *to do*. Let's call all of these positive commands and directions the *white*.

There are also in the Scriptures an array of things which obedient Christians are told *not to do*. Let's call all such prohibitions the *black*.

But in addition to these white and black activities

covered by specific positive or negative scriptural commands, there is also a vast array of present-day activities that are not mentioned in the Bible. These are usually things on which even professing Christians hold differing views. Let's call these the *gray areas.*

Does the Bible offer guidelines for these gray areas? Can sincere Christians know what they ought to do—even though there is no specific "Thou shalt" or "Thou shalt not" in God's Word? Most confidently they can.

In God's divine wisdom He has provided *principles* that, in the absence of specifics, do give clear guidelines to any Christian who truly desires to know and do God's will.

Guidelines for the Gray

These guidelines for the gray areas are in four different relationships: to one's self, to one's Christian brothers and sisters, to one's circle of influence and to God. The Christian who would know God's will in the gray areas must earnestly and honestly follow these principles:

First, *the Christian must not do, or willingly permit, anything that harms or defiles his or her body or dulls his or her love and loyalty to the Lord.* "Do you not know that your body is a temple of the Holy Spirit, who is in you, whom you have received from God? You are not your own; you were bought at a price. Therefore honor God with your body." (1 Corinthians 6:19-20).

Second, *the Christian must do nothing—even if it does not bother his or her own conscience—that will hurt, offend or weaken a Christian brother or sister.*

Be careful . . . that the exercise of your freedom does not become a stumbling block to the weak. For if anyone with a weak conscience sees you who have this knowledge eating in an idol's temple, won't he be emboldened to eat what has been sacrificed to idols? So this weak brother, for whom Christ died, is destroyed by your knowledge. When you sin against your brothers in this way and wound their weak conscience, you sin against Christ. Therefore, if what I eat causes my brother to fall into sin, I will never eat meat again, so that I will not cause him to fall.
(1 Corinthians 8:9-13)

We might paraphrase a much-used expression and say, "Let *their* conscience be your guide." That's a good rule of thumb when it comes to gray areas.

Third, *the Christian must permit into his or her life nothing that will hurt, hinder or cause to stumble those within the sphere of his or her influence.* "Let no debt remain outstanding, except the continuing debt to love one another, for he who loves his fellowman has fulfilled the law. . . . Love does no harm to its neighbor. Therefore love is the fulfillment of the law" (Romans 13:8-10). "You, my brothers, were called to be free. But do not use your freedom to indulge the sinful nature; rather, serve one another in love" (Galatians 5:13).

Fourth, *the Christian must do only those things that, in every area of life, will glorify God rather than to bring reproach upon the name of Jesus Christ or damage to His reputation.* " 'Everything is permissible'—but not everything is beneficial. 'Everything is permissible'—but not everything is constructive. . . . So whether you eat or drink or whatever you do, do it all for the glory of God" (1 Corinthians 10:23-31).

Four Questions

Based on those guidelines, four questions, honestly faced, will enable a sincere person to make a judgment about any activity. Here are the questions:

1. Does this activity in any way harm my body, the temple of the Holy Spirit, or weaken my love for the Lord?

2. Does this activity, though it may not trouble my own conscience, hurt or offend in any way my Christian brothers or sisters or lead them to engage in something that may cause them to fall?

3. Will engaging in this activity "turn people off" to the Lord because of what they consider to be my questionable behavior?

4. Will my involvement in this activity bring glory to God, or will it dishonor His name and hurt His reputation?

Such self-questioning needs to be done in total honesty. Unfortunately, people's approach to questionable things appears to be "Why *can't* I?" instead of "Why *should* I?"

The Questions Applied

Many of the activities mentioned earlier simply won't stand up to these four questions. Take, for example, the commercial theater. Some time ago I made an informal survey of the movie ads in the leading newspaper of a major North American city. Over those weeks of my survey, I found less than 10 films among the dozens advertised that were classified for family viewing. I found even reading the advertisements a distasteful experience. Vi-olence, blatant sex, crude humor, outright mockery of righteousness, even blasphemy abounded.

How can any person who claims to have the Holy Spirit within him or her, who claims to be controlled by the Holy Spirit go to see the kind of mental and moral garbage the ads lead a person to expect? It is incomprehensible. Unless a person attends the theater very, very rarely, he or she has to be exposed to that filth, for there simply are not that many decent pictures.

Admittedly, there has been an effort recently to produce some films that *are* acceptable entertainment. Even these need to be carefully evaluated lest they subtly promote a non-Christian world-view.

The application of all four principles and questions, in the light of the content of current films (and most TV programs and many commercials) precludes Christian viewing.

Application

As to social drinking, David Wilkerson in his extremely well-documented book, *Sipping Saints*, proves that there was—and is—a non-intoxicating, nonalcoholic wine in the Middle East. The argument that the Bible endorses the use of alcoholic wine just does not stand up. And, anyhow, an honest application of principles one and two particularly will have an effect on a believer's participation in or rejection of social drinking.

Popular music, most of which, according to one magazine's report, is tested in a notorious New York City homosexual establishment to determine its "popularity potential," certainly has a dubious claim upon the Christian. Any believer who will sincerely apply the principles will not spend time, money and interest in such pursuits.

The list could go on. When Christians wear many of the current and often extreme fashions, they violate the second principle through "defrauding"— the arousal of desires within others which cannot be righteously fulfilled—something expressly forbidden in God's Word.

Smoking? Well, even the governments of the United States and Canada demand that every package of cigarettes and every cigarette advertisement carry the warning that smoking is harmful to health. No question here for the Christian! The very first principle puts a ban on smoking.

Do you know what disturbs me most? I sense that many people of all ages, but especially young people, seem determined in their "Christian liberty" to see just how close to the world they can come, how much like the world they can be, without losing their Christian life and faith.

They seem to have forgotten the words of God: "Do not love the world or anything in the world. . . . Everything in the world . . . comes not from the Father. . . . The world and its desires pass away, but the man who does the will of God lives forever" (1 John 2:15-17).

There's great danger in seeing how close one can get to evil. It just doesn't make sense if a person wants to do God's will and pursue holiness.

A Key Point

A good many years ago the owner of a stage coach line which ran through the Rockies advertised for a driver. It was a dangerous job because of the hazardous mountain roads and steep cliffs. But the job paid handsomely because of the danger and the requisite skills.

A crowd of applicants showed up. The owner interviewed each one individually. The key point of the interview came near the end in the form of a question.

"How close," the owner asked, "can you come to the edge of a drop or a cliff and still maintain control of your stage coach?"

The responses varied. Some drivers boasted that they could come within a wheel-width or less. One even allowed he could "hang a wheel over" and still be in control! One man answered differently.

"I really don't know how close I could come," he replied. "You see, in my driving I concentrate on staying as far *away* from the edge as I possibly can."

He got the job.

The Christian whose life is really going to count for God is the one who will set himself or herself to honestly apply the principles that govern the "gray areas." He or she will stay "as far away from the edge" as possible. "After all," the Bible comments, "it is not for nothing that the Spirit God gives us is called the *Holy* Spirit" (1 Thessalonians 4:8, Phillips).

"Make every effort . . . to be holy," we read in Hebrews 12:14; "without holiness no one will see the Lord."

Legalism? No!

License? Definitely not!

Lordship? Yes! With Jesus Christ in full control through the divine power of the Holy Spirit, you'll know what to do about the "gray"!

CHAPTER	Holiness,
29	the
	Experience

by H. Robert Cowles

EXPERIENCE—ALREADY YOU HAVE SPIED
the red flag. "Don't rely on experience; it is
not dependable." " 'We walk by faith, not by
sight.' " "Never trust experience."

But we do trust experience! All of us do. And that is
part of our problem in this matter of holiness. We
have generally shaped our teaching of holiness and
our standards as to what constitutes a holy life by
looking either at our own experience or at someone
else's.

Even when we consult the Scriptures, it is usually
to cite the experience of the 120 in the Upper Room
or Peter's radically altered behavior (experience), or
Paul's amazing missionary achievements (experience). I repeat: When it comes to holiness, experience—our own or someone else's—becomes
our paradigm, our model.

And the seeker after holiness likewise looks at
these examples, whether biblical, in church history
or contemporary, and thinks, *There is a person who
represents the ideal in holiness; I should expect as
much in my life.*

Who Comes to Mind First?

Of all the people in the New Testament, who comes to your mind first when someone mentions being filled with the Holy Spirit? If you didn't answer "Peter," I am curious to know whom you put ahead of him!

Peter. The Day of Pentecost. A sound like the blowing of a violent wind. What looked like tongues of fire resting on the assembly of 120. Suddenly, everyone declaring the wonders of God in the everyday languages of fellow Jews from all over the Roman Empire visiting Jerusalem at that festal time.

And there is Peter, standing up with the Eleven: Peter, ever the spokesman for the apostles, Peter addressing the excited, mystified crowd that has quickly gathered that morning. And by the time he has finished his Spirit-anointed message—all of it extemporaneous—these Jewish visitors are under deep conviction. They are begging Peter and the other disciples, "Brothers, what shall we do?" (Acts 2:37).

That was not human persuasion. It was Spirit persuasion. That day, about 3,000 people were added to the 120 original believers.

Nor did it stop with the passing of Pentecost. Peter, the pace-setter, and John are on their way to the three o'clock prayer time at the temple. There at the Beautiful Gate is a mature man who has never walked. *Never.*

We are not informed if Peter and John made the prayer meeting. Having ministered divine healing to the handicapped man, they were caught up in another excited crowd of curious onlookers.

Another impromptu sermon turned curiosity into conviction—and faith. Church membership figures bulged once again (Acts 4:4).

We Jump to Conclusions

What have we been looking at? Experience. Holiness, the experience. And what is our conclusion? Of course, we would not cast it in such explicit terms, but the thought is subliminally there: *Holiness, sanctification, the filling of the Spirit, the empowering of the Spirit—use whatever term you prefer—enables a person to bring people under conviction of sin, enables a person to win multitudes to Christ, enables a person to minister healing to the physically handicapped.*

If Peter, our Exhibit A, is not sufficiently convincing, there are others: Stephen, the first martyr; or Paul, the indefatigable missionary and writer; or John the beloved, who authored one of the Gospels, three of the New Testament Letters and the Revelation; or James, half-brother of Jesus, later leader of the Jerusalem church and probably the author of the Letter bearing his name.

These are blue ribbon manifestations of holiness, the experience. And if we dare admit it, *our* experience of holiness doesn't stack up very well against those. *We* are not on the front lines 24 hours a day doing battle for God. *We* haven't founded a dozen churches. *We* haven't written any Gospels.

The conclusion is self-evident, inescapable: If *we* were full of the Holy Spirit like they were full of the Holy Spirit, we would be accomplishing what they were accomplishing.

A Few Questions

But before we get too carried away by that line of reasoning, we should ask a few questions concerning the Bible record. Peter, John, James, Stephen and Paul we admit to being acquainted with. And Barnabas. Silas, except for his singing in the Philippian jail, remains obscure. Apollos, Aquila, Priscilla are shadow figures. Likewise Titus and Timothy, Philemon and Onesimus.

We've named a baker's dozen of post-Pentecost people. We may be reasonably familiar with no more than half of them—meaning we have enough information about them so as to form some fairly accurate assessment of their personalities and their activities.

But what about the other nine or ten apostles? What about the other 117-118 people on whom the Spirit fell at Pentecost? What about the 3,000 who were converted and Spirit-filled that same day? Or the thousands of others mentioned later in the Acts? People were being added to the church not weekly but daily.

What also about the Gentile believers, starting with Cornelius? They peopled the dozen or more central churches that Paul and his associates founded and possibly hundreds of satellite offshoots of the major congregations.

What I'm saying is that we base most of our concepts of holiness on the experiences of half a dozen people who admittedly did great exploits for God, but who may not—who probably do not—represent a cross-section of all the Spirit-filled believers in the post-Pentecost decades of the New Testament era.

Moreover, we tend to look at this half-dozen un-realistically. It's a well-established phenomenon that we tend to screen out the disagreeable from our memories. We recall the savory aroma of grandma's stove-baked bread; we screen out the back-breaking loads of firewood we carried to heat the oven. We long for the old homestead on the hill; we momen-tarily forget it had neither inside plumbing nor electric lights.

It can be that way in our assessment of people we greatly admire. We reflect fondly on their many good qualities; we down play their few, albeit pos-sibly significant, faults. We overlook the warts.

Idealistic Terms

There is yet another factor that comes into play. Paul, James, Peter, John, in writing their letters to New Testament Christians, tend to promote holi-ness of life and character in idealistic terms. "The fruit of the Spirit is love, joy, peace, patience, kind-ness, goodness, faithfulness, gentleness and self-control" (Galatians 5:22-23). "No one who is born of God will continue to sin. . . . He cannot go on sinning, because he has been born of God" (1 John 3:9)."Just as he who called you is holy, so be holy in all you do; for it is written: 'Be holy, because I am holy' " (1 Peter 1:15-16).

We look at such elevated Scriptures and we tend to suppose the primary recipients already were near those goals. We forget that in actuality they were people who could be (and were) divisive, selfish, unruly, legalistic and of sometimes faltering faith.

Even the Spirit-inspired writers themselves were not quite perfect. Paul and Barnabas had their sharp disagreement over John Mark (Acts 15:36-40). Paul tangled with Peter over the latter's hypocrisy (Galatians 2:11-13). And these are the elite, the cream of the crop.

What should we conclude from the *other* 117 in the Upper Room, the *other* 3,000 Spirit-filled Christians from the Day of Pentecost, the massive number of *other* respondents as "the Lord added to their number daily those who were being saved" (Acts 2:47)?

It is, of course, dangerous to argue from silence. We do not *know* if the other apostles had ministries as fruitful as those of Peter, John and Paul. If church tradition is at all accurate, they, too, made their marks in areas as diverse as India and North Africa. The Scriptures inform us that the intense persecution following Stephen's martyrdom scattered the Jerusalem Christians widely, and they "preached the word wherever they went" (Acts 8:4). We know from reliable early writings that these first- and second-generation believers impacted their world for Christ.

The Record Is Impressive

We are impressed by Stephen, by Barnabas, by Phillip and even by second- and third-generation Christians such as Timothy.

Origen (185-251) would later write: "In all Greece and in all barbarous races within our world, there are tens of thousands who have left their national laws and customary gods for the law of Moses and the Word of Jesus Christ; though to adhere to that Law is to incur the hatred of idolaters, and to have embraced that Word is to incur the risk of death as well. And considering how in a few years and with no great store of teachers, in spite of the attacks which have cost us life and property, the preaching of that Word has found its way into every part of the world, so that Greeks and barbarians, wise and unwise, adhere to the religion of Jesus—doubtless it is a work greater than any work of man."

Tertullian (160-240) said to the Romans: "We are but of yesterday, and yet we already fill your cities, islands, camps, your palace, senate and forum. We have left you only your temples."

By A.D. 313, 5 to 10 percent of the vast Roman Empire was Christian. Perhaps 50 percent of Asia Minor, Thrace and Cyprus was Christian. Important segments in Antioch, northern Syria, Egypt, Rome and proconsular Africa were Christian.

The conclusion is inescapable. Those early Christians may not all have matched Paul or Peter or John for achievement, but they far outstripped the *average* professed Spirit-filled believer of today. We can only pray as the Welsh sexton prayed following the revival in Wales, "Lord, do it again!"

Let Others Say It

One other observation is appropriate to an essay on holiness, the experience. Maybe I have overlooked something, but apart from one Old Testament prophet in the midst of his prophecy (Micah in Micah 3:8), I cannot recall a single person in the Bible declaring, "I am filled with the Spirit." It was said about a number of people, beginning with Bezalel, the tabernacle artisan (Exodus 31:3). Luke notes that Stephen was "full of faith and of the Holy Spirit" (Acts 6:5). He informs us that Barnabas likewise was "full of the Holy Spirit and faith" (Acts 11:24). Perhaps God intended for holiness to be assessed objectively rather than subjectively. The person who boasts, "I am Spirit-filled, I am holy" finds it hard to sound convincing.

I can claim to be Spirit-filled and holy, but if my wife or children, who see me day in, day out, have a different opinion, their assessment carries the greater weight.

In our earlier years, my wife Marge and I did a lot of disputing. For that I accept the blame. I tend even yet to be legalistic and vindicatory. Be that as it may, in 1970, I became aware of a distinct change in my wife. All the old arguing had evaporated. There was peace and harmony between us. There was tranquility in our home. Life was serendipitous. As I reflected on the preceding months, I could not point to any crisis in her life that might account for so subtle but welcome a change.

More than a little amazed, and at a loss to explain it, I confronted Marge with my awareness of this new atmosphere in our home.

"Marge," I said, "you've changed. We don't argue like we used to."

"*You've* changed!" Marge countered. "Ever since you came back from the Canadian revival."

I thought back to that weekend, several months before, in Saskatoon, Saskatchewan, and specifically to the Sunday evening service. It was held in the city's largest church. Still there were wall-to-wall people as that entire metropolitan area was stirred to its very roots under the Spirit-anointed ministry of Lou and Ralph Sutera and the other participating ministers. I had found a seat high up in the balcony, and we were singing Fanny Crosby's great hymn,

"Draw Me Nearer." The second stanza goes:

> Consecrate me now to Thy service, Lord,
>   By the power of grace divine;
> Let my soul look up with a steadfast hope,
>   And my will be lost in Thine.

Somewhere in the middle of that second stanza, standing far up there in the gallery of a normally cold, formal church, this one-time missionary-turned-administrator-turned-magazine editor quit being a reporter of the revival and became, instead, a participant.

There was no sound like the blowing of a violent wind, no tongue of fire. But God quietly did something new in my heart. I was not even aware how great was the change. But Marge saw it.

Hearts Purified by Faith

Peter made an interesting and significant comment as he addressed the first Jerusalem Council. He began by reminding the delegates that "some time ago God made a choice among [them] that the Gentiles might hear from [his] lips the message of the gospel and believe" (Acts 15:7). His reference, of course, was to the conversion of Cornelius, the Roman centurion, and his household. Peter continued: "God, who knows the heart, showed that he accepted them by giving the Holy Spirit to them, just as he did to us. He made no distinction between us and them, for he *purified their hearts by faith* (15:8-9, emphasis added). As Peter spoke, a score of years separated him from that special day of Pentecost when he and the other apostles had been filled with the Holy Spirit. Over the years some of the details of that event had faded—the sound of wind, the tongues of fire, the languages in which they glorified God. But one detail remained fresh in his mind: *Their hearts had been purified by faith.* They had been made holy. They had been set apart for a holy God's holy service.

> *Are you longing for the fullness of the blessing*
>   *of the Lord*
>   *In your heart and life today?*
> *Claim the promise of your Father, come*
>   *according to His Word*
>   *In the blessed old-time way.*
> *He will fill your heart today to overflowing,*
>   *As the Lord commandeth you,*
>   *"Bring your vessels, not a few";*
> *He will fill your heart today to overflowing*
>   *With the Holy Ghost and pow'r.*
>   (Lelia N. Morris)

We are called . . . to be . . . separated from the spirit of the world even as Christ is not of the world. There can be no holiness without this.
—A.B. Simpson—

	Julie Fehr,
CHAPTER	a Holy
30	Woman

by Lisa Rohrick

SCATTERED THROUGHOUT THE RAIN-FORESTED hills of southern Gabon in equatorial Africa are the villages of the Tsogo (SOH go) tribe. As a young missionary living among the Tsogo people, Julie Fehr (rhymes with *Care*) struggled to learn Getsogo, their bubbling, vowel-filled language.

Though she put in the required hours (and more) of language study, it simply did not work for her to sit at a desk and laboriously memorize grammar charts and lists of words. She had to spend time around the village fires carefully listening to and imitating the sounds she heard. She had to be with the people.

Several months into her language study, Julie had an opportunity to spend three days in a village a few miles from where she lived. A colleague going in that direction offered to drop Julie off and pick her up on the return trip. It would be a chance for Julie to immerse herself in the Getsogo language and put into practice the phrases she had been learning.

Alone!

Julie had visited this village and others many times, but this would be her first overnight stay. Fear and excitement mingled in her heart as the sound of the four-wheel-drive faded into the jungle, leaving Julie a lone Westerner with her three boxes of luggage.

Wanting to take good care of this visiting "white child," the chief and his wife vacated their house for her. Faces filled the doorway and windows as Julie began to unpack her belongings. Julie suddenly realized how awkward her situation was. In Gabon, no African woman would be permitted to travel without her husband or children. Julie was a single woman—a category of person that didn't even exist in Gabon—except for prostitutes!

As Julie slowly set up her table and camp stove, many pairs of eyes followed each move. She tried in her limited Getsogo to follow a conversation between the chief and a village elder. She knew they were talking about her being alone. She was quite sure they were talking about her needing company for the night. She tried to explain to them that she was not alone because God was with her, but she felt she wasn't getting through.

With heart racing, Julie resumed her unpacking, hoping the novelty of watching her set up her camp cot would bring about a change of subject. As she slid the poles of the cot into place, she heard shouting out in the courtyard. Several times the phrase was repeated before Julie caught what was being said.

"It's a one-person bed! It's a one-person bed! She

brought her own bed, and it's only wide enough for one person!"

Some time later, Julie overheard a Gabonese Bible teacher scold the villagers for even thinking that she would want male company for the night. "She is *God's* woman!" he told them in no uncertain terms.

God's Holy Woman

Early in her missionary career, Julie chose two Scriptures to guide her life. The first was Joshua 24:24. The Israelites told Joshua, "We will serve the LORD our God and obey him." The second, which she often quoted, was Romans 12:1-2, where Paul directs his readers to "offer your bodies as living sacrifices, holy and pleasing to God." It was Julie's deepest desire to be holy and pleasing to God.

As Julie went from one Tsogo village to another, teaching the words of God, people watched this white woman. They watched, and they saw that her actions told the same story as her words. She talked about a God who loved her and who had saved her. She explained that she wanted to live according to God's rules. She told them that God loved them and could save them from the evil spirits they feared.

Julie told them things about God that were written in the Book she carried. She told them about His power. He was stronger than the evil spirits. They saw that she believed in the strength of this God. She did not carry any of the fetishes they used to protect themselves from danger and sickness.

Julie told the Tsogo villagers about the rules God wrote down for people to follow. They watched as she set an example for them. On Sundays she wouldn't use her truck to help people haul sand or work with them in their plantations. This, she told them, is because God instructed people to have one day a week as a holy day, set apart from the others. But they also learned that God was not unreasonable in His rules. If a goat fell in a pit on a Sunday, one could pull it out with a clear conscience.

Genuine Love

Julie taught the Tsogo villagers about God's love for them. But her message was not merely words. She lived what she said. As God's ambassador to the Tsogo tribe, she too loved them. If ever they had wondered about her love being genuine, they knew it for sure when Chief Tanga died.

Chief Tanga, small in stature, was the leader of a comparably small domain consisting of one suburb of Yenu, a collection of villages where Julie often taught. Ten years before Julie set foot in Chief Tanga's village, Enoch, a Tsogo Bible teacher, had visited there.

"Get out of my village!" the chief ordered. "The words of God will not be taught here. Get out!" Enoch got out. Ten years later he returned, accompanied by Julie.

This time the chief grudgingly called his villagers together and allowed the visitors to teach. But when they prayed he bowed neither his head nor his heart.

Several months later, Julie was in a neighboring village. She was preparing to return home after some days of teaching when a messenger reported that Tanga wanted to see her. She went.

Tanga told Julie he was sick. He had gone through

all the sorcery treatments he knew. Still his illness remained. He wanted Julie to take him to the mission-run dispensary.

"Promise me you won't have anything else to do with sorcery," Julie bargained. "God will not mix His medicine with Satan's." Tanga agreed, and Julie took him to the dispensary.

Weeks passed, and Chief Tanga's health returned. He went home on foot, declaring to his family that he was well, detailing the wonderful treatment he received at the hands of Julie and her coworker Clara Lou Stucky, who ran the dispensary.

A Tragic Outcome

Back home, Tanga's family agreed that he was much better, but they insisted that the treatment begun at the dispensary must be "completed." Tanga bowed to their pressure, going with them into the forest to resume the sorcery he knew he should leave behind.

On her next visit to Tanga's empire, Julie could not believe that the sick, bloated man she greeted was Chief Tanga, who had walked away from the dispensary only a month earlier. Her heart was heavy as she heard from the Christians in the village how Tanga had returned to his old ways.

In the kitchen of Tanga's house, Julie sat quietly as family members defended their decision to "complete" Tanga's treatment. Tanga said nothing; he knew he had done wrong. Finally, Julie had heard all she could take.

"You are mocking God!" she declared, interrupting their excuses. "You are making His work a plaything!" Tears began to roll down Julie's cheeks. The family sat stunned. They had never seen a white woman cry.

"People of this village," Julie continued, "change your thoughts! Turn your hearts to God!" Then she left, overwhelmed with sorrow and confusion, fearing the villagers would interpret her tears as anger.

Two days later Chief Tanga died—without Christ. That afternoon Julie sat again in the kitchen of Tanga's home with the village women, and they cried together. The following morning, before leaving for the next village, Julie went to say good-bye to Tanga's widows and the women with them. One asked Julie to say a few words to them. Another began to question Julie's right to address them, but the aunt in charge spoke up.

"I saw this one weep for Tanga," the woman said, referring to Julie. "She wept for him when he was still alive, weeping for his illness. Tears fell from her eyes yesterday as we wept over his death. He himself said there is no person like this one."

Not many in Tanga's village knew Christ, but they saw His life and His compassion in this white messenger who cried real tears when their chief died. They saw a life that was being made holy by the Spirit of God.

A New Name for Julie

One day as Julie and Enoch were on their way to visit some of the villages of Yenu, they stopped to give a ride to an elderly couple who were on their way home. It was Tobacco, the chief of another suburb of Yenu, and his wife. When they let off their two passengers, the little wife looked at Julie and asked, "What is your name?"

310

"Sair," Enoch answered for her, using the Tsogo pronunciation of *Fehr*.

"But don't you have a *real* name?" the woman persisted.

Julie didn't know how to respond. "Sair" was a real name as far as she was concerned! She paused and looked at the woman questioningly.

"Well," the woman continued, "know that your name is *Monyepi*. I've named you Monyepi!"

Enoch asked Julie if she was willing to accept the name. Julie readily agreed. Who wouldn't want to be Monyepi, which means "beautiful one" or "lovely one"?

Tobacco nodded his approval. "It is a good name for you," he said. "My wife and I had a long walk home with our baskets, but you made the trip *beautiful* for us!"

Tobacco also was pleased to have Julie and Enoch teach the Word of God in his village. In fact, he invited her to return and stay for several days, which she did a month later.

Tobacco's wife was glad to see Julie. "Monyepi," she called out, "come and greet me!" She reminded the villagers that Julie had a *real* name, which they all began to use.

Language Help and a Good Samaritan Role

At the time, Julie was translating the New Testament into Getsogo. So she sought help from some of the elderly villagers for words she needed. Particularly she was looking for a word or phrase to translate what Paul terms his *manner of living* or *way of behaving* among the Thessalonians (1 Thessalonians 1:5) and before Timothy (2 Timothy 3:10). One old man spoke up.

"Monyepi," he said, "that's why you got that name. It's all part of the name. It's not only the way your teaching makes God's words attractive to the people, but the way you live also beautifies the Word."

God was making Julie into a holy woman. And these Tsogo villagers had taken notice.

Doing the right thing was not always Julie's natural response. It was an Easter weekend. Julie and several others were involved in a youth camp that had been in progress all week. Each evening they showed the *Jesus* film, drawing large crowds from the community. In the first five nights 95 people had received Christ Jesus into their lives. Now Julie had pulled up to the church for the final showing of the film. As her passengers were getting out of her truck, two young men ran up to her.

"Please come with us," they panted. "Our sister is in labor. Please take her to the hospital!"

Julie was tired. And there was an ambulance in that city. Surely they didn't need her that badly. But then she remembered the good Samaritan. She had seen him in the film five times that week! She couldn't say no. So she got back into her truck and picked up the expectant mother for the trip to the hospital. It soon became obvious that the baby was not going to wait for a hospital delivery. Julie pulled over to the side of the road. There in the front seat of her truck she delivered the baby!

Proceeding on to the hospital, they located a midwife, who took over, and Julie excused herself to return to the church. She got back to her standing-room-only place at the church just in time to see, for the sixth time that week, the good Samaritan befriend the injured Jew.

Cancer

In June, 1994, Julie took a break from her work as missionary scholar-in-residence at the Billy Graham Center in Wheaton, Illinois, to attend the General Assembly of her church held that year in Toronto. For several weeks she had not been feeling well. As soon as the Assembly concluded, Julie entered a Toronto hospital for extensive tests. The finding: incurable cancer.

Early in the morning of July 3, Julie wrote in her journal for the last time: "Romans 12:1-2—for how many years have these [verses] guided my life? That does not change now. Even though my body is full of death cells, multiplying at their own murderous pace, this body is still a living sacrifice which I can intelligently give to the God of my life."

Two days later Julie had surgery for what the doctor termed an "aggressive and widespread cancer," much of which he was not able to remove. It was cancer of the gallbladder, very rare and not responsive to treatment.

In the weeks following her surgery Julie talked freely of dying. Often she referred to Paul's words in Philippians 1:20-21: "I eagerly expect and hope that I will in no way be ashamed, but will have sufficient courage so that now as always Christ will be exalted in my body, whether by life or by death. For to me, to live is Christ and to die is gain."

The Sacrifice Is Complete

Two weeks after her surgery, Julie had regained

enough strength to be transferred to a hospital in Langley, British Columbia, where she could be near her family. Often those who visited her were cheered themselves by her positive disposition and grateful attitude.

"God is so good!" she remarked repeatedly. She was grateful for an adjustable bed, pillows, a fan. She was grateful for family and friends who loved her and tried to make her comfortable.

Julie suffered intensely, but there was peace and beauty in her face as she asked for prayer that she wouldn't let her Lord down amid the pain. The same holiness observed by the Tsogo villagers was evident to the medical staff in Langley.

On August 30, 1994, Julie Fehr's living sacrifice was at last complete. She passed beyond suffering into the presence of her Lord, Jesus Christ.

God, who had made her holy, must have been well-pleased with His handiwork.

God is now aiming to reproduce in us the pattern which has already appeared in Jesus Christ, the Son of God.
—A.B. Simpson—

Participating
Authors

Participating Authors

Rev. Wallace C.E. Albrecht is Vice-President, Personnel/Missions in Canada.

Dr. Keith M. Bailey, pastor, church administrator, conference speaker, lives in retirement in Dayton, Ohio.

Dr. Paul F. Bubna is Vice-President, The Christian and Missionary Alliance, and President, Alliance Theological Seminary, Nyack, New York.

Dr. Arnold L. Cook is President, The Christian and Missionary Alliance in Canada.

Rev. John A. Corby, Jr., is Field Director for France.

Rev. H. Robert Cowles, retired missionary, editor, executive, lives in Carlisle, Pennsylvania.

Dr. Arnold R. Fleagle is Senior Pastor, Stow (Ohio) Alliance Fellowship.

Dr. K. Neill Foster is Executive Vice-President/Publisher, Christian Publications, Camp Hill, Pennsylvania.

Rev. Armin R. Gesswein is Founder/Director, Revival Prayer Fellowship, Inc., San Juan Capistrano, California.

Dr. William R. Goetz is Senior Pastor, Hillsdale Alliance Church, Regina, Saskatchewan.

Rev. Robert B. Goldenberg is pastor of Community Alliance Church, Wickenburg, Arizona.

Rev. Wendell K. Grout is Senior Pastor, First Alliance Church, Calgary, Alberta.

Rev. Fred A. Hartley, III, a popular author, is Senior Pastor, Lilburn (Georgia) Alliance Church.

Dr. Maurice R. Irvin is Editor, *Alliance Life,* and a sought-after conference speaker.

Mrs. Joy Jacobs is a popular author and conference speaker. She and her husband, Robert, live in Dillsburg, Pennsylvania.

Mr. Fred S. Jennings, an Akron, Ohio, businessman, is President, Alliance Men.

Dr. Thomas B. Kyle is a national evangelist. He lives in Milaca, Minnesota.

Rev. George S. Liebmann is Senior Pastor, Pinewood Alliance Church, Longview, Texas.

Rev. D. Paul McGarvey is Superintendent, Western Pennsylvania District.

Dr. Gerald E. McGraw is Director, School of Bible and Theology, Toccoa Falls (Georgia) College.

Rev. Angel V. Ortiz is Superintendent, Spanish Western District.

Dr. John E. Packo is Senior Pastor, New Hope Community Church, Miamisburg, Ohio.

Dr. David L. Rambo is President, The Christian and Missionary Alliance, Colorado Springs, Colorado.

Miss Lisa Rohrick, a missionary candidate, is a graduate of Canadian Theological Seminary, Regina, Saskatchewan. Her home is in Invermere, British Columbia.

Dr. David E. Schroeder is President, Nyack (New York) College.

Dr. Albert B. Simpson (1843–1919) was founder and first president of The Christian and Missionary Alliance.

Mrs. Charlotte Stemple, former missionary to Vietnam, is President, Alliance Women.

Dr. A.W. Tozer, pastor, conference speaker, was Editor of *Alliance Life* until his death in 1963.

Rev. Kevin L. Walzak is pastor of Alliance Bible Church, Culpeper, Virginia.

Dr. Donald A. Wiggins is Assistant Vice-President, Division of Church Ministries, and President, Christian Publications.

Rev. W. Robert Willoughby is Minister-at-Large in Canada. He lives in Stoney Creek, Ontario.

> *Note: All of the authors are related to The Christian and Missionary Alliance.*